Sonny and Me + Redd

Sonny and Me + Redd

Gene Anderson

Copyright © 2025 by Gene Anderson

All rights reserved. No part of this book may be reproduced in any manner whatsoever without written permission except in the case of brief quotations embodied in critical articles and reviews.

The people, places, and events in this book are the recollections and opinions of the author. There is no ownership or relationship implied for any company, song, album, brand, trademark, or other intellectual property, except as explicitly stated by the author during the time period referenced, to the best of his memory and knowledge.

Every effort has been made as to fair use of the photos or composites in this book, owned or believed to be owned by the author, or with no other claim of ownership known, and with credit given when known.

Transcribed by Clarice Carolyn Jones
Additional edits by Rita Parker, RP Confidential LLC

First Printing, 2025
Amorphous Publishing Guild
Buffalo, NY

CONTENTS

Introduction 1
Sonny's Light 2
Checking In 18
Beyond the Ring 23
Golden Nights 42
Geney Boy 63
Trip to Rueben's 72
Band Reunion, then Down to Two 85
Sonny's Story 101
Hollywood Road Trip 106
Sonny's Shadow 129
Bad News 136
Every Day is Christmas 142
The Big Chance 150
Red's House Parties 160
Alone in Hollywood 169
Epilogue 172

Introduction

Sonny Liston, known as the greatest heavyweight boxer, died in 1971. Liston's death left the world with speculation even after the coroner of Clark County reported Sonny's death was of natural causes. It was reported by others that Liston's death was of a heroin overdose. Now, after years of unfounded truth, Sonny's one and only true and trusted friend, Gene Anderson, shares the truth of his life with his friend Sonny Liston, and how it resulted in a relationship with eccentric comedian Redd Foxx.

Sonny's Light

Me and Sonny. It is Charles "Sonny Boy" Liston, prized fighter, good friend, and a very controversial person. Meeting him changed my life and it has never been the same.

I met Sonny by a fluke. I just happened to be walking down the street back home in St. Louis one fall evening and my cousin, Marvin Louis, ran from out of a storefront. She said somebody wants to meet you. I went back into the office and there were a bunch of old guys in there, old gangsters, old police, old ex-police inspectors and just tough old guys. They had wanted me because they had seen me on TV, doing some of the songs I had recorded. Somebody recognized me, so I went in there with them. We got to talking and they all had big pistols hanging out their back pockets. There was one guy who was the ringleader, the boss of all the old gangsters. His name was Lou Powell. He was once an inspector for the police department who had retired, and he was involved with the local politics and lot of little deals that was big to me at that time. And there was another big police in there by the name of Mr. Troup, who was an inspector or captain or something like that. They were big guys in town, and I had heard about their reputations as a child growing up and it was like man, these is the big boys.

In the course of the conversation, they started talking to me about being an entertainer and what I had done. My cousin, Marvin Louis, had already hyped them up on me because I guess I was the pride of the family. I had done so many things. I had sung with David Gallespie, I had sung with Duke Ellington, and I traveled across country, had been in the Army, things like that, so my folks was proud of me. The neighbors and the entire community was familiar with what I was doing and my activities, so these guys were familiar with who I was, and they just wanted to just say hello. But in the process, I looked behind Mr. Powell's desk and I saw an almost 50-by-100 huge photograph of him standing up with Sonny Liston, holding his hand up in the air and it had the heavyweight championship belt.

I said, "Man, Mr. Powell, do you know Sonny?"

He said he did.

I said, "Is it possible you could introduce me to Sonny because I want to meet him?"

I wanted to meet Sammy Davis, Jr. at that time because I had seen an article in Jet magazine where Sammy Davis, Jr. was trying to rejuvenate Sonny's career. He was acting as some kind of manager for Sonny at that time. Mr. Powell looked at me and he spoke up and said hell yeah with a very crusty old voice with a cigar hanging out his mouth with his bald head shining with half his hair pulled over from the side over the top of the bald spot on his head, boy he was a tough looking old guy but he was a sweet old guy, he said "Yeah kid, I know that Sonny Liston, the son of a bitch owes me money, you want to meet him."

My eyes lit straight up. This is an opportunity. I was looking at Sonny standing there holding his hand in the air. Mr. Powell got the belt, and Floyd Patterson was over in the far corner with his head hanging down where Sonny had just beat him for the championship and that was the talk of the entire town. Sonny Liston won the championship, a St. Louis boy, now the heavyweight champion of the world.

Here's a chance with guys that know Sonny and here is a chance to meet my hero, and Sammy Davis, Jr.. Sammy Davis, Jr. was to me how Michael Jackson was to the youngsters of this era. "Mr. Powell can you hook it up?" I was so enthusiastic all the other gangsters just burst out laughing. My cousin Marvin Lewis looked at me like, yeah that's my cousin y'all. I was so excited it took me a moment to try to get out, you know, out the office, I was asking a million questions, so it finally boiled down to Mr. Powell told me that when Sonny was coming to town pretty soon to have a small town fight at the Kill Auditorium to pick up a little extra money and that when he comes to town he would introduce me to Sonny so just stay tuned. In other words, I was happy with that man, I rushed home and told everybody, man, I just met Mr. Powell, Lou Powell.

My folks looked at me and said you met who? I said yeah… I said Mr. Lou Powell.

They said, "Man, what you doing with them gangsters?"

I said, "Well I don't know if they gangsters or not, all I know is that they know Sonny Liston and Sonny is going to come to town and I'm going to see if I get to meet him and if so I might talk him into introducing me to Sammy Davis, Jr.. And from Sammy Davis, Jr., I know he get a chance to meet me and know how much talent I got, he could see himself in me and well, heck, I might get the chance. I could be able to do some big things for all of us."

You know at that time I was freshly married, I had a young wife, a young baby, with my sister, my nephew, we all was living in a small apartment upstairs over my daddy's tavern. My daddy had a tavern called International Hookup on Martin Luther King Drive and we was all staying up there with my mom and like I was trying so hard to get something together so that I could move us on up. I was trying to do something big so I can help my mom do some big things, you know, cause I had it in me, my heart was there, I really believed that at that time for sure that with the talent that I felt that I had. I could do it. All I need was just a break and this look like this could possibly be my break.

One thing was that I had already goin' around the world singing with a duet called Sam and Bill. I had taken Bill Johnson's Place. Bill Johnson quit the group with Sam Gray, and Sam Gray didn't want to act right – you know he was shooting dope – and I wasn't into none of that. I was like a star athlete. I didn't want to do anything but sing and dance and turn flips and do splits and stuff and make people happy. I thought I was doing it good, because I had been around the world and traveled with the Temptations, traveled with Junior Walker and a lot of the Motown Acts. We had done tours with and met a lot of stars since I had gotten out the Army. I got with Sam as soon as I got out the Army.

It took me a year to get back home from traveling on the road, so I was a very seasoned entertainer and that was even before I met my wife and got married and we had a baby. My whole life was closing in on me, so I was trying to put all the pieces back together and to see if I could get back on that professional status, so I was working hard. I formed a group. I had a new band. I had a few new records that I had recorded on my own, cause I had been under contract with Chess Records with Sam as Sam and Bill and they put us on the shelf 'cause the Chess Brothers – Lenny and Phil Chess and them, and Max Coopersteen, those guys over there – they was upset with Sam because they had spent that money on us to go on to Chicago, to go on and record. And Sam – he stayed high all the time – we could never get anything out of us, so it made no sense, so they just wrote us off.

So I had already spent a year just calling them every day, "What you gone do about the record? What you gone do about the record?" We cut some good records but they just didn't want to spend no money on us so they just had Ramsey Louis, Fauntela Bass, Lil Milton, bunch of big name stars over there, they didn't really care about us after they found out that it was a bad investment. Besides, Sam was the true leader and he was the one that they had negotiated with so talking to me wasn't what they really wanted to do. And I stressed out so much about it, so getting the opportunity to meet Sonny Liston so I can get to meet Sammy Davis, Jr. was to me at that time was a golden opportunity. So I went home and I told my wife, I told my mom, I told all the fellas in the band that I had met some people that was going to introduce me to Sonny Boy Liston, and they was going to see if Sonny would introduce me to Sammy Davis, Jr., which at that time as I said was my absolute hero.

Well a couple a weeks or so passed by the one day I got a phone call from my cousin Marvin Louis, he said Mr. Powell want to talk to you. He came to the phone and with his crusty old voice he said, "Aye kid, Sonny boy be in town next week. He's going to be at the Southside Gym and I want you to get over there and hurry and I want to introduce you to him." Somehow I think this is the right thing to do, coming from a guy like Mr. Powell that was all the encouragement I needed 'cause I know that he didn't fool around — if he said it, it's going to be true.

Two weeks or so passed by — sure enough I get another call from my cousin Marvin Louis, cause he stayed with those old guys at the time 'cause they was on top of the political heap in St. Louis, and Marvin Louis always stayed with movers and the shakers, and he was also a police officer with the St. Louis police department. So I got in my old car – I think I had a Ford, I don't remember it was an old clunker – I jumped in the car and went over to the Southside Gym.

Man, I was dressed back in the old 60s days, the hippie look with the Jimmy Hendricks look I guess, with the big long collar shirts and the chains and the platform shoes, and my hair was hanging all down like a wild rock and roll singer too, and if you would've seen me at that time there would've been no doubt this is a true entertainer.

Man, I walked into the Southside Gym, they was boxing just like in the movies — like you would have seen it in the Rocky movies. The guys were punching bags here and punching bags there. Guys were sweating. You could smell the men in the gym just like a movie. Man, I was so excited cause I hadn't been in no gym like that. I remember when I was a kid I was in small-time Golden Glove gym but this was the real big league gym for professional fighters. There I saw my cousin Marvin Louis, he was begging for me to come back there in the little small office area looking like they had fixed it up for a make-shift private dressing room for Sonny Liston.

I walks into the room and everybody was whispering quietly, you could hear the voices murmuring real low as if everybody was afraid to speak up. I comes into the room and there I saw him, sitting in a corner way back in the room. It was a small tight room and he was wrapping his hands slowly; he was sitting on a stool and looking at me as 'what is this that just walked into my dressing room' and I was so young and so energetic and so happy to be there, I almost just exploded.

I came out loud and clear, "Hey, Sonny, I'm Gene Anderson — they call me Petey."

Everybody in the room just bust out laughing and Sonny had the kind of laugh, like sniggling himself. He said, "Petey"...

Mr. Powell, Lou Powell, stepped up, said "Yeah, Sonny, this is the kid that I was telling you about. The boy has got so much talent, he's the one that wants to meet Sammy. I told him I was gone see if you could try to hook him up with Sammy."

Sonny looks at me and he looks me up and down, he said "What do you do?"

I looked him just as brassy and proud and said, "I'm the best entertainer in the city of St. Louis — I can dance, I can write, I can sing, I can make people laugh, I can make people happy, and I can do what I do as good as you can do what you do."

He said, "You know I was heavyweight champion of the world..."

And I said, "Well, I'm the heavyweight champion of St. Louis entertainment."

He just bust out laughing, apparently that was the first time that they had a very warm moment in that gym since he arrived there because Sonny was known for staring his opponent down and being so serious about everything that everybody round him was just afraid of him even those that was close to him. Everybody was afraid of him except Mr. Powell. Mr. Powell wasn't afraid of nobody not even Sonny boy. Then he looked up and he asked me, "Well if you that good, I'll keep you myself instead of giving you to Sammy."

And I told them "Well it don't make me no difference, somebody do sum with me because I'm tired of being here in St. Louis and I ain't getting nothing coming I don't beat everybody doing everything here in St. Louis, I'm the best entertainer — can't anybody outdo me in this town, and I'm just fed up with it and I'm ready to go. Man gimmie a shot, somebody help me..."

He burst out laughing then he say this kid got balls, aint he, so we all kind of like laughed and joked around until he said, "Well everybody get out of here cause I got to get my mind together to go out here and train for this fight coming up." So we slowly staggered out the room and that's when I got a chance to meet all the guys that was his entourage, that was some people that end up actually historical people. At that time I just thought they was just regular ordinary guys that was with the training camp, so Mr. Powell took me around and introduced me like I was a grand nephew of his to all of the people that he figured I needed to know.

I got a chance to meet the legendary Dick Sandler who was at that time Sonny Liston's manager. He was also the manager of the newly crowned Olympic heavyweight champion George Forman, and Sonny's heavyweight sparring partner at the gym. He used George Forman for the heavy fighting and some more guys for the punches. Shytes at that time was a former lightweight champion boxer who helped Sonny develop his speed because he was a fast mover. He also used Shytes so he could get his reflexes up to speed. Little did anyone know that years later that George Forman would end up the heavyweight champion of the world. Shytes was the manager that brought Foreman back to gain the heavyweight championship of the world after he lost to Muhammad Ali. He retired for all those years, and he came back almost three-hundred pounds but somehow Shytes got him in shape by using the old routines, I believe. He became the world heavyweight champion for the second time in his career and became the most lovable person.

At that time, Foreman was mean and evil just like a wannabe copy of Sonny Liston. He had his mouth turned down and looked like nothing was ever funny. He was just looking at you as if, "Boy, you say anything to me ill break you in half." I didn't say anything to him. When Sonny came out the dressing room, he climbed up slowly to the ring and the reporters started to flashing camera lights because he was still a big celebrity in St. Louis, especially because he was a homeboy just returning back home for a fight and it was a big deal. I'm looking around and there are gangster-looking guys. There was David Runnion-type characters, mafia guys. There was the big White guys out there with the cigars.

"Hey Sonny boy," he waves at them, holding his head up like a champion and stuff then the bell ring finally. I never saw him in George Forman's spot, never saw that but I know that was the purpose of him being there. He and Shytes got in the ring together and Shytes was hitting him (bat, bat, bat, bat, bat, etc.) and Sonny hit him (pat, pat, pat, etc.) and they were shuffling around real good. I saw some fancy moves Sonny had that was real slick. He hit Shytes (bam) really quickly and knocked Shytes down on the floor (bloop). He said, "Oh, boy I told you get out the way." Then everybody burst out laughing.

Oh, Sonny was a character. So, they sparred around for a little longer and he skipped a little rope, and he did the medicine ball. Then he did the shadow boxing and whatever the routine was they went through it. I followed them step-by-step. I was behind him just like a tail on a donkey, man. He was looking back at me like man, what you want, you still here? I was right behind him. Yes Sonny, come on baby. I just pepped him up a little bit.

I'm pumping him up and I'm having a great time. I'm have the time of my life. Everybody looking at me like, man, leave Sonny alone and let him train. I wasn't thinking about what they was talking about. Somehow, he kept looking over at me laughing and he boxed a little bit harder. Seem like we had bonded right at that moment you know. He didn't like that people would be afraid of him deep down inside, especially those that was around him supposed to be friends. He knew that their relationship with him was not a true relationship. Those that was really free with Sonny, really just had a true friendly aura around him he really appreciated. I found out that in the long run as time went by and I got to really know Sonny.

So, after the training was over, we all got into the limo and went to a restaurant to get something to eat. It was me, George Forman, Shytes, Dick Sandler, Mr. Powell, my cousin Marvin Louis, and I think it was somebody else. It was a big, long stretch limo and we was going to some big Italian restaurant, something that some gangsters owned. They had invited Sonny over there with his entourage for dinner, so you know

I was sitting there like trying to figure out like, am I dreaming? Is this true? Was I really with the great Sonny Liston? And I'm riding with them known mob guys? I'm surrounded by all these heavy dignitaries and these old gangsters like Mr. Powell. Man, I'm in the middle of the whole game right now. What's going on?

So, as we were riding down the road it was a little bumpy here and there. Everyone was quiet, and my mind was running a thousand miles a second. George Forman was popping gum. Sonny turns around and says, "Aye, spit that gum out. Poppin' that gum is bothering me." George kept on chewing and popping the gum. Sonny turn around and said, "Hey, did you hear me? I said spit that gum out, it's bothering me." George Forman says to Sonny, "Sonny, boy if you seen the way I whooped that Russian in the Olympics you wouldn't talk to me like that." Sonny turned around, he looked George Forman straight in the eye and said, "I aint that Russian. I'm Sonny Liston. Spit that damn gum out now!" George Forman looked at him a second, rolled the window down and spit the gum out the window.

That was a very intense moment for me, especially a guy looking at all these iconic people around me. I was a young rookie that don't know anything but thinking to myself, wow ... all this drama. Everybody in the car just froze for a moment and finally we reached the restaurant. We had dinner and the mob jumped out, reporters jumped out saying, "Hey, Sonny boy." They are taking pictures, and he is looking at everybody like man I'm so tired of this shit I don't know what to do. That seems to be what was on his mind, but he was a diplomat. He knew how to play the game, so he threw a few little fists up in the air like most champions do. Threw a few kisses and he had me sit down beside him.

He said, "Hey kid, sit by me Geney boy." Wow, that was what I call a real moment in my life, so I went home and told everybody what happened. Man, I been to the gym with Sonny Liston he said he gonna try to help me meet Sammy Davis. He told me I could even be with him and things if I look like I was good enough. Aw man, I was just filled to the top with excitement about that day. My cousin Marvin Louis had finally hooked me up with all the prominent people in town that I needed to know. Now I had something to hold on to other than just the frustration of what went wrong with the record deal and me and Sam. That was the closest thing I had to the big time since I had gotten out of the army.

Soon the big fight came, and it was down at the Kid auditorium. They were talking about it on the television, the news, on the radio and everything. They were saying that Sonny's having a big fight at the Kid auditorium tonight and who was going to win and all the celebrities that were coming to town to see the fight. Man, I was excited. I said I didn't get a ticket; I didn't get any passes, I didn't know anything about none of that at the time. All I knew was that I was supposed to go. Nobody called me to say the fight is going on at the Kid auditorium tonight. What am I going to do? I knew today was the only day it was going to be possible to get with these guys cause after the fight was over, they were going to go back to what they were doing. I don't have addresses. I don't have any phone numbers. I don't have anything, no information except the fact that I was with them at dinner and saw them talking. Man, it's got to be something bigger than this cause I done told everybody that I'm going to get with Sonny.

You know, they hyped me up a little bit about the whole story. Nevertheless, the fight was tonight, and I had to figure out something. So, I thought I'll just go and see if I can get in and tell them I'm with the Sonny Liston entourage. Tell them anything but just go. I had just bought a brand-new linen white suit. I put it on with my white fedora hat, jumped in my old hoopty, and rolled down as fast as I could to the Kid auditorium. I got down there and it was so packed and there was no place to park. All the parking lots was full, and all the meters was full. The car was so old I didn't really care at that time, so I just pulled it up on the sidewalk right in front of the entrance door.

Nobody was out there, no police, no ticket takers, nobody. It was a ghost town outside, but inside the arena it was jam-packed. Since there was no place to park, I just got out of the car and said, forget about it.

I run to the door, and nobody stopped me at the ticket office, so I walk straight on up the ramp. One, two, three ramps and next thing I knew I found some doors. Nobody was at the door, so I opened the door and there was a crowd screaming and hollering. I was at the top of the arena, and nobody was taking tickets. Everybody was busy looking at the fight. Being a brassy young guy that I was, I didn't care no way, so I just walked on in. When I walked in, I looked around and nobody said anything to me. I walked down the first flight of stairs or so and there was a little partition. I stepped over it went down on the next flight and looked around and nobody said anything, so I stepped over that partition. I did this all the way down to the main floor and nobody stopped me.

I'm saying wow, look at my luck. Everything is going great. Man, the crowd was electrifying, people was screaming and hollering. That's when I saw Sonny in the arena fighting with this guy, beating up on each other. They had been fighting like you wouldn't believe for seven or eight rounds. They was leaning up against each other. Both of them was tired and sweating and Sonny hitting him, (boom, boom, boom, etc.). One throw, slow blow, boom. Another throw, a slow blow, and clenched all up every now and then. They would throw a jab then boom, and they was fighting in slow motion. They was both tired and they beat each other really badly. I was so excited! I was at my very first big-time fight, and nobody stopped me. I walked up closer and closer and before you know it, I was at ring side. Right by the ring listening to the commentators announcing the fight. Looking at the big guys with the scoreboards and everything and the seconds in the corner with the grease and the spit bucket stuff. I'm saying wow, I'm right here. Everybody looking at me didn't know me because I got this beautiful white suit on and I'm lit up under the light as if I was a big-time manager or something. Man, I'm walking around there like a gang cop. Got my chest stuck out and I'm just almost throwing my hand up like I'm the heavyweight champion of the world. I'm having an exciting time. This was quite an adventure for a guy of my young age.

All of a sudden, the bell rings and they went back to the neutral corners and sat down. I walk over to Sonny's corner, and I look at him. He don't pay me any attention at first. He did not see me reach up under the ropes in between the guys that was wiping him off, hosing him down, squeezing the water all over his head, making him breathe, getting him structured. I grabbed him by the trunks, and nobody said anything.

I pull on his trunks, he looks down at me and he said, "Hey Gene baby, what you doing in here?"

I said, "Champ, you mean you gonna let him do us like that? I ought to get in there and kick your ass myself. You know you can fight betta than this."

He fell out laughing right on the stool.

I don't know what happened, but it must have exhilarated him. He got right up and took a big deep breath. The bell rang and he ran out there and started pounding on this guy like you wouldn't believe. BOOM, BOOM, BOOM, BOOM, BOOM, BOOM! People started screaming and hollering. "RUN FELLA! RUN GUY! RUN! SONNY'S GONNA RUN YOU"! Boy, Sonny boy was hitting him here and there, just beating him up against the ropes and beating him against the wall. The next round he came down there and said, "How you like that kid?" I say, "Look at you. That's what I'm talking about. Don't you make me get up there and whoop your ass." He busted out laughing in the middle of the fight.

He went out there for the next two rounds or so and beat this guy to a pulp. They almost had to ring the bell to stop the fight. In the end he won the fight by unanimous decision. Boy, I was so happy I was screaming and hollering. I walked around there as if I was like, look at what we did. Walking toward the dressing room he said, "Aye, Geney baby, I'll see you at the hotel." He told one of the guys in his entourage to give me a note saying meet them at the Roosevelt Hotel, downtown St. Louis. Sonny boy want to see you man. That was a great moment for me.

Then it came to me, MY CAR! It's downstairs on the sidewalk! I knew that I had to hurry up and get down there quickly. I couldn't hardly get past the people. The people was trying to pat me on the back after seeing me down there with Sonny. "Aye boy, y'all did good." They thought I was part of some entourage. What I'm trying to do now is get outside, save my car from being towed off the sidewalk because what am I going to do? That's all I got is the little ole raggedy hoopty. I finally got a chance to get there and there my car was, sitting there as if nobody wanted to take it. Nobody wanted to see it, and nobody wanted to tow it, and I started it up and the smoke shot out the back of it as if it was a choo-choo train.

I headed straight to the Roosevelt Hotel. I got there a little sooner than he did, so I hung around in the lobby in hopes that I could see him and his entourage when they walked into the hotel. Then we could get together and talk about this meeting with Sammy and him. Since he had won the fight, I know he should be in great spirits by now. I waited and I waited but he never showed up. I kept walking around, looking in different places where I thought he may have been. Maybe he's in the lounge, maybe the restaurant. I looked everywhere and there was no Sonny, so I began to get really frustrated with the issue and sort of sad. This looked like this was the end of my encounter with Sunny Liston.

I got ready to go then out the clear blue sky the elevator came down and there he was, dressed to a T. Man, did he look good. He always wore those big fedora hats, the big ones. He had on a plaid sport coat, some Serge pants, some Stacy Adam shoes. Boy, people was just waving at him, and he was throwing kisses up like the champion does, and he was with the most drop-dead gorgeous blonde I had ever seen. Back in those days, Black guys with gorgeous White women was very, very rare especially in a town like St. Louis, Missouri. Then he saw me. "Gene baby, I was hoping I was gonna see you." This is what he said, and my face lit up, my heart jumped. I was just so happy he didn't forget me. Man, he was the champ that remembered me!

He grabbed me by the arm and introduced me to his girlfriend. Her name was Barbara, a beautiful, tall, blonde young lady who was a Las Vegas cocktail waitress. She had befriended Sonny and became his girlfriend, and she was a model, and she was drop-dead gorgeous. He has somehow worked out a deal and put her on the front page of Vogue magazine. She was famous and everybody was talking about her.

I didn't know about all of this. All I know is that it was Sonny and his girl and man, she was a sweetie pie as a person. First thing she did was stuck her hand out there and her hand felt just like it was velvet, it was so smooth. She said she was so glad to meet me. I looked at her like I couldn't believe my eyes because she was just so unbelievably beautiful. All I could think about was wow, look at Sonny's girl. Man, this is the champ. This is the champ for real. We sat down and he bought a couple of drinks. I sit there and I talk, talk, talk, talk, talk. He laughs, laughs, laughs, laughs, laughs. She laughs, laughs, laughs, laughs, laughs. I was having the time of my life because it seemed like when I got round Sonny, I got happy. I would say things that I normally wouldn't have said just to keep him laughing. I just kept him laughing. He had one of the most infectious laughs in the world. Throughout our entire life I could always make him laugh, even when it was at very, very, very, bad moments. I could still make him happy and make him laugh because I really became a loyal friend to Sonny and he became a real true friend to me.

As we talked, I began to explain to him all the things that I had been through and all the things that I wanted to do and all the things I thought I could do. He was very impressed with the confidence that I had in myself and that I really felt in my heart that I was that qualified. Somehow, I impressed him with the fact that I felt he was the type of person that would give you a shot. Sonny always gave people breaks and shots in certain things in life. No one really would have an idea how generous he was, trying to help other people. He knew he had such a reputation of being such an evil, bad, mean, or unsavory person. None of that, *none of that* was true about the real Sonny Liston.

Somewhere within the conversation Barbara spoke up and said, "Sonny, this kid looks like we should try to help him if we can."

He said, "Do you really think we ought to?"

She said, "Yeah Sonny, I think that we need to try to help him out if we can find something for him to do, if he could ever get to Las Vegas."

I said, "Well Sonny, I can get anywhere you want me to go if you have something you can hook me up with."

He said, "Well I tell you what I'll do."

He reached in his pocket, and he pulled out a book of matches. On the back of the book of matches he took a pen, and he wrote his phone number down and then he handed it to me. I looked at it as if it was platinum diamonds. I was like, this is Sonny Liston's personal home phone number. Man, I was just flabbergasted with the thought that he thought that much of me that he would give me that phone number. Sonny, in my eyes and most of St. Louis' eyes was a big hero. So, we talked about it a little longer and I decided to go and leave them alone and let him party with his girl. I didn't want to overstep my welcome because I already had gotten more than I expected to get.

Before I left, he said, "Hey listen kid, don't forget to gimme a call sometime. Hold on to that number."

I said, "Hey champ, there's no way I'll lose this number cause I'm gonna learn it."

He busted out laughing and I busted out laughing, then she busted out laughing. I threw a thousand kisses and ran out the door with a smile on my face as big a jack-o-lantern. I had been successful. I met a friend who was a world-famous figure, Sonny Liston, and I was on my way sooner or later to Las Vegas to meet my idol, Sammy Davis, Jr..

Checking In

Two weeks passed by, and I decided to give him a call, check the number, and see if the number was for real. I called, "Hello..." It was Sonny, I couldn't believe it. I said, "Hey Sonny boy, this is Gene Anderson."

He said, "Gene baby, I was hoping I would hear from you. I was wondering what happened to you."

I said, "Well man, I just wanted to wait a little while before I called you."

He said, "What can I do for you?"

I said, "Man, I just wanted talk to you about what's going on out there in Las Vegas."

I tried to explain to him that the band had abandoned me and gone somewhere in Colorado to some army base. I was there struggling, tryna get something done but I'm still cutting records. So, he said, "Well aye, I'm going to get you hooked up with some people. You can talk to them, and they can find out some way to bring you out here and do somethings cause it's a lot of things going on out here. So, you need to try to work your way out here so you can have some ideas to take back there and do some new things."

I said, "Okay, Sonny, I'll call you back again later."

So, we had this same type of conversation four or five separate times, but I'd always call him just to freshen his memory about me. Who I was and some of the things I wanted to do, that we both could be a part of, and I just needed to get out of St. Louis and try to better my life. He could understand that cause when he was living in St. Louis, he had major problems here. He wanted to stay in St. Louis, but they wouldn't let him. The police stayed on him, kept badgering him and he couldn't get no place, couldn't get no opportunities. He was with the mob, jail, all kind of changes here in St. Louis so he knew the stress I was under, especially back in those years. So, he sympathized with me. He told me "If you ever get the chance come, I gotchu."

So, one day by some stroke of faith, I got a TWA getaway credit card in the mail. Till this day I'm still tryna figure it out. I never applied for it. Maybe my ex-wife applied for it or something. I don't know but during those days my marriage was getting kind of rocky. Everybody around me seemed to be wanting to use me because I was making a few little records. They wanted to use me for their own personal purposes and stuff like that. I wasn't really enthusiastic about being in St. Louis. I was trying to figure out a way to still help my family get out of this poverty mode. If I could get out of St. Louis and to Las Vegas where Sonny was and all the things he had told me about, and all the people he had put on the phone with me, that may have been some help to me. If only I could get out there and start a new life, then I could reach back and help everybody around me that I loved, and all things would be well. That's what I thought...

So, I started to make preparations for getting out to Las Vegas one way or another. I made up my mind that I was gonna go and I called him one evening, about 6 or 7 o'clock and I said, "Sonny I'm gonna think about coming out there."

He said, "Well listen, don't keep talking about it, do something about it. Come on if you coming and I'll see you when you get here." He said it real casual. He didn't have the faintest clue that I had made up my mind and I was on my way right then.

I already had a lot of new uniforms, costumes, and new street clothes of that era. It was the bell-bottom era with long-collared shirts, capes, bone glasses and boots. I had all that kind of stuff that no one had ever seen before because we were creating them at that time. Bell-bottoms was never in the stores and people didn't know about that stuff. All they knew was that it was strange-looking. Guys that was dressed in strange looking ways, popping up here and there. Some in San Francisco, Memphis, Florida, St. Louis, Chicago, and Detroit. Just popping up wearing these funny looking new clothes that everybody excited about when we showed up in them. I had a lot of them. I had all colors, all kinds, all kinds of material. I had a special tailor to make me these special looks that no one else had ever seen before. The flashy look was something that I was a master of, so I packed all that stuff up.

I told my wife what my plan was, jumped on an airplane and before you knew it, I was on my way to Las Vegas. I was so nervous and filled with anxiety about arriving there for the first time. I had never been to Las Vegas. I always wanted to come. I heard about how it was so glamorous with so much glitter. So much excitement going on and gambling, the show girls, the big bands, the money, the live entertainment. All of the stars were there, man.

It was my opportunity. I was on my way, and I was not gonna fail. I was not gonna take no for an answer as far as me being able to conquer this town. I was pumped up and motivated and I also had a real friend there that was somebody, Sonny Boy Liston. I can't express how optimistic I was about my future. I just knew this was gonna be it. I got my family behind me. The whole town knew I was gonna leave and go out there and be with Sonny Liston.

I had interviews on the radio and did a little small TV show and that's all I was talking about, pumping it up. Then I was finally on my way. I got on the plane, and I was telling people that I was going to Las Vegas. I was gonna make my fortune, I was gonna do good. I had my little raggedy guitar with me and man, I was so decked out that people wanted to know, "Who are you?"

"I'm Gene Anderson. I'm gonna be one of the greatest stars that Las Vegas have ever produced." I just believed that in my heart and I was saying it to people. They were laughing but they believed it too. Man, I was so happy I was on top of the world.

I remember it was 12 midnight when the plane took off. A little later, when we got to Las Vegas it was just a little after 12 midnight again. I didn't know that there was a such thing as time change, so I thought that something was wrong with my watch. I was walking around, and people were busy talking and making reservations. It was exciting for me. I had never experienced anything of this electrifying magnitude before. All I could think about is I finally made it to Las Vegas ... where is Sonny?

I ran to the phone booth, dialed the number and a sleepy voice said, "Hello."

I said, "Sonny boy it's Gene."

He said, "Gene baby, I just got through talking to you."

I said, "I know it but guess what? I'm here."

Sonny said, "You here? What you mean you here?"

"I'm here in Las Vegas at the airport, come pick me up."

He was overwhelmingly excited and not believing that I had made my mind up after all this time of talking back and forth. He said with excitement in his voice, "I'll be right down to pick you up Gene boy, I'll be right there." Sonny was the type of guy if you really wanted to do something he always wanted to help. A lot of people thought that Sonny was a selfish person. I never saw a selfish side of Sonny. He was always there to help people. He would buy shoes for kids, he would take old ladies to buy their groceries and stuff. Sonny was a good guy if he thought you weren't trying to use him.

So, it wasn't very long before I saw big commotion at the front door of the airport. Back in the 60s, Maclaren [McCarran] was a small airport, and it was sort of intimate. I looked and there Sonny was. He walked through the door looking like a mountain, he was so huge. Everybody was gathering around him, and people were taking pictures. Sonny Liston, Sonny Liston, Sonny Liston! Man, some people was scared; some people was acting like they knew him and he was walking through the crowd as if they was even there looking for me. And he had on a Kelly green dot ring Italian silk suit with some dark green alligator shoes and a red and green fedora hat. Man, he looked like a big, huge star, looking great.

He saw me and broke into a big smile. He said, Gene baby!"

I said, "Sonny boy!" I ran across and dropped my bags.

Man, I hugged him, and he hugged me and said, "Boy, you got heart, didn't expect you to get here and here you are."

I said, "Yeah Sonny, I'm here Sonny boy. Let's do it."

He didn't even help me with the bags. I had two big gray bags full of clothes. He just walked in front of me and started waving his hand at people and people just gathered around him. He was just being Sonny Liston, the champ of the world. He used to say to me I should've been with him when he was champion. Well, back then I couldn't imagine what that would've been like with him being champion. At that moment that was a lot of excitement for me, for a country boy who had finally made it to the big time. The biggest name that I had ever been with, Charles Sonny Boy Liston, the former heavyweight champion of the world — not the United States, but of *the whole wide world*.

Beyond the Ring

When we left McCarran Airport, went into the parking lot, and there it was — a long, green Fleetwood Cadillac with a black vinyl top. Man, we were in style.

I felt like I had finally arrived in heaven and was with the biggest guy I had ever met. I was with Charles "Sonny Boy" Liston, the former heavyweight champion of the world. As far as I was concerned, he was still the heavyweight champion. I was walking with a legend. I had heard so much about him and there I was, on my own now. I knew it was official because I was in Las Vegas.

We got in the car, and he was so friendly to me it was like I was a long-lost son that just arrived, and he had been waiting for the longest. I never knew until the end that Sonny was very lonely. He was looking for people that really loved him or liked him for him as a person, not for what he could do for them. In his heart he knew he was a good person. He knew I was just young, green and really just enthused. Even though he knew I wanted to meet Sammy and further my career, he knew in his heart that I was happy right there being with him.

First, he showed me the strip. It was nighttime, close to midnight. I'm sleepy, I'm ready to go to bed, I'm used to being asleep at that time of night, but this is Las Vegas. Las Vegas back in those days was wide open like the gates of hell. Everything was going on. We finally made it to the strip because it was a lot of desert out there then. It wasn't building on top of building like it is now, it was a lot of just raw desert coming from the airport until you hit the strip. We came in off of Tropicana Boulevard and that's where I saw the top of the strip, which was the Tropicana. Man, it was a great big, huge blue fountain squirting up water and it was the biggest thing I ever seen. All I ever seen that had squirting water was the Union Station down in St. Louis and it had a little fountain that we would swim in when we were kids. This was a big, huge fountain and neon lights were everywhere.

I would look down the street and he would ask, "How ya like it kid?" I couldn't even speak. I was just totally flabbergasted. You could see in my eyes that excitement was running straight through my veins. It was like I couldn't wait to see what the casinos looked like. I wanted to put it all on red like I had seen in the movies. I wanted to bet the little hundred dollars that I had burning a hole in my pocket. I knew I was going to be lucky and win at least half a million dollars. That was just a young, naive country boy's dream. Nevertheless, I sure had it in my heart I was gone try.

Sonny was staring at me knowing it was my first time in Las Vegas. He knew what was on my mind so he kind of like smiled a little bit and we got out of the car. That's the first time I had ever seen valet service. I had seen it in the movies but I'm actually living and receiving valet service. We jumped out of the car and people looked at us like these must be some big-time guys because Blacks at that time was held down to a Jim Crow style. Their attitude was strictly "if you were Black stay back", but Sonny was an exception. He wasn't allowing none of that to happen to him. He wanted to do his thing the way he wanted to do it, and nobody could tell him anything. They had learned that by the time I got there with him.

Sonny Liston's car had hardly stopped before bell hops was right there, Mr. Liston this and Mr. Liston that. People finally figured out that's Sonny Liston, the heavyweight champion of the world. Girls started coming up to him, tourists started coming up to him asking for his autograph. It kind of like made him feel good cause he was showing out for me. I knew this because he was just signing his name very slow and looking at people saying nice little things to them. I knew that wasn't the Sonny Liston that they had told me he was like. They said he was rough and tough enough that the whole wide world was afraid of him. But this was a whole other story. He was being a diplomat, a legend, being a star. He was being all of the things.

I was just so proud to be there with Sonny, it was like it was a dream. I told myself it has got to be a dream. I'm here with Sonny Liston, people are wanting his autograph, they want my autograph. Wow, not only the bell hops but everyone in the casino. The bosses was saying, "Sonny boy!" He was throwing his hands up like the champion he was. I was walking with my chest stuck out saying, "yeah that's us, aye Sonny boy that's us!" Man, I was so excited, I felt like a kid in the candy store. Man, the lights was bright, and I had never seen that many lights burning in one building before. I never seen those cocktail waitresses with the little, short miniskirts. Miniskirts was just getting to be the fashion statement for the era in those days.

Sonny started introducing me to pit bosses, and the crap dealers, and the blackjack dealers. "Hey, this is my boy, Geney Boy. He's my new artist from St. Louis. We gonna do some big things with this kid so I want you to meet him." They started to shake my hand. Man, I started to feel like I was a real dignitary. I looked around me and I didn't see that many Black people. I wasn't accustomed to that because my whole world had been around militants. That was sort of like I was hanging out with H. Rap Brown and all the Black storm rangers. I didn't know anything about the total integration of things in this big-time super world of Las Vegas. At that time, I really felt kind of strange, but I had no fear, no apprehension. I only felt good about certain things because I was with Sonny Liston. I felt as long as I was with Sonny, the whole world was wide open to whatever I wanted to do.

He tried to convince me that as long as he was there with me don't worry as long as it made some sense and we could look like gentlemen. Now that was kind of strange because Sonny had a reputation of a wild bull in a China closet at certain times. I found out in the long run it was very true but at certain moments in Sonny's life he was very calm, very serene, and very diplomatic.

So, we walked into the show, the first time I had ever been to a Las Vegas big lounge show. In those days the lounges had super acts that everybody wanted to see. You had people like Sammy Davis, which I was so destined and die hard to meet. You had people like Nipsey Russell. You had people like [The] Four Stepbrothers, The Nicolas Brothers, Check Mate, Count Basie, O. C. Smith. Most of these guys was lounge acts back in those days. That's what I was hoping I was going to get a chance to do. This is what Sonny and I had discussed on the phone, about maybe getting me to open up a show for one of these big acts in the lounge.

So, we walked through the doorway of the show room and the Maitre'd walked up and said, "Hey Sonny boy, what's up?"

Sonny said 'hey' to whatever his name was. He said, "I got my boy, Geney boy from St. Louis. I want to let him look around and see what the shows look like, is that ok?"

He said, "sure Sonny boy, come on in".

He parted the curtains and there it was, like a musical that was in the movies that I had seen as a child. Fred Astaire and Ginger Rogers with the show girls dancing around them. There was a guy, I think his name was Domenico Modugno. He was a big Italian singer, and he wrote great songs Dean Martin would sing. Tony Bennett sang Dancing in the Dark. Aw man, they had wonderful show girls with the feathers in their hair and the feathers hanging down their butt. The fans in their hands and the titties was out. There was rows and steps, and steps and rows, and rows of long leg, beautiful White girls with big titties.

Tony Bennett just pushing your eyes out as he walked down there in a white, long tail Tuxedo singing Dancing in the Dark. I said in my heart, hell yeah that's me one day. I didn't realize that Sonny had been pulling on me and pulling on me saying come on let's go. I'm still flabbergasted; I'm stuck like a truck looking at these titties. I got to get some of this for me, man. My mind was running a thousand miles a second. Sonny and the Maitre'd laughed they ass off when they saw me. I'm steady trying to look back and he's pulling, but I'm saying, "but Sonny, but Sonny".

He said, "Come on Geney boy, it's more titties down the street. Come on boy!" I bust out laughing, he bust out laughing, the Maitre'd bust out laughing. He was able to eventually pull me out of there.

Man, I was so excited and there was no doubt about it, Sonny Liston had proved himself to be my main man. After he showed me around the place a little, we went back out to valet parking. The guy had Sonny's car parked right by the curb. He didn't have to go back into the garage or over to the other parking area where the other valet was. He was right there at the door. Sonny tipped him a five-dollar bill which was a lot at that time in the 60's. Man, one dollar was a lot of money to me, so we was rolling like Batman and Robin.

We went across the street to an old casino that they eventually tore down. I think they named it MGM, but then it was a casino named The Bonanza. It was built like a big Indian reservation where all the girls looked like Pocahontas. They wore Pocahontas buckskin miniskirts while waiting on the tables. Every guy was in buckskins, dressed up like Indians.

So, we pulled up and people started gathering around Sonny like he was like Michael Jackson. That's probably why he stayed in Las Vegas, because people respected him for being the champion of the world and not all the other types of things. People were saying he was with the mob and stuff like that because at that time the mob was running this whole town. We walked through the Bonanza, and I fell in love at first sight with the first Pocahontas I saw. The dress was so short I couldn't believe it. Man, I had never seen miniskirts this short. Titties was puffed up in the air and they was so smiley and up in your face and I'm saying 'hey baby' to everyone. Sonny is laughing his ass off. He said, "boy you are having a great time, aren't you?" I have never done this before. He said that's okay kid, do your thing I got your back. Go ahead and do what you want to do.

I was hitting on one little waitress. I can't remember her name now but somehow, she gave me her phone number. She said, "Hey cutie pie, I kind of like that outfit that you got on." The outfit that I had on at that time Miss Geneva Spikes made. It was vinyl, but it looked like leather and had brown alligator type pants with bell bottoms. The vest with a diamond in the back had a cape with a yellow satin lining, and a yellow satin ruffle front shirt with ruffle sleeves. Man, I had the same kind of leather cap on and bone on sunglasses.

Man, I was doing it up, trust me. I was looking like a real player of that era, and I was looking like an actual stock entertainer. I had saved up and got right to go to see Sonny. He was proud of the way I looked because, as I found out later, the Black guys in Las Vegas was being held down. They were treated in a subservient, stereotype manner that was associated with the deep, deep South. They kept all the Black people totally segregated back in those days except the stars, the millionaires, and the world-renowned celebrities like Sonny. That might be why he really did like me so much. He knew I had no fear or that Jim Crow type attitude around me because I had been part of the civil rights activist era for so long and was so prominent in it. I was hoping to have a confrontation so I can let them all know that you can't treat me like this. I'm not going to take it and maybe that was why we had such a major bond because he was very rebellious when it came down to that. Sonny's greatest hero was Jack Johnson who as you know was very defiant when it came down to what he could or what he could not do on the strength of his race.

Sonny didn't take anything off nobody, but when he was sober and in his right frame of mind, he was such a gentleman. People just loved being around him. He would make it plain and clear to me over and over again to be a man and stand up for what you believe and don't let them run over you. So, as we moved along, I got the girl's phone number. I showed Sonny he said boy, you quite a little ole playa ain't you? I said nah Sonny boy, I'm just with you man, and I know that I can get away with anything. He busts out laughing. He said don't you fool around and get whipped and we both just fell out laughing.

I asked myself how they gonna whoop Sonny Liston? This is the heavyweight champion of the world. They can't whoop the champion. Little did I know that he was still just a man just like us.

We walked down to another lounge where it was a band playing and very few people. It was a smaller band from Texas or California. The reason I remember so well is the leader of the band was the famous disc jockey named Wolf Man Jack. Wolf Man Jack was one of the best early disc jockeys that played R&B music that stretched all the way across the United States. Some other syndicated affiliates were John Richbourg and Horse Man Alan. These were the pioneers of soul and R&B music. These disc jockeys got the music famous.

I think his real name was Bert Silverman or Sugarman, something like that [legal name, Robert Weston Smith]. Anyway, he could not sing a lick, but everybody knew who he was, so they was applauding. The band was absolutely the bomb they could play like there was no tomorrow. There was pumping and humping but he couldn't sing his way out of a wet paper bag. Everybody loved it because that was still Wolf Man Jack. He had a voice like Louis Armstrong when he talked.

Come to find out that all was a stage act. He never talked like that even though he was famous for talking on the radio with that Satchmo Armstrong voice. He was a typical man just like an insurance salesman with phony hair, phony sideburns and mustache and beard. He was completely a fake, but when you saw him, it looked like it was real. I had a chance to see him later on in the game and he didn't have that stuff on. Sonny told me that's just make up that he puts on and I couldn't believe the famous Wolf Man Jack was running with a disguise on. He was living two lives.

Sonny introduced me to him, and I saw it with my own eyes. Sonny and he were very good friends. He mentioned Sonny's name, so he stood up and raised his hand like a champion fighter. He finally came down offstage to sit down with us. Sonny introduced me as Geney Boy.

That's the first time he really started to call me Geney Boy. "He's from St. Louis and he's a singer." He said, "I want to bring him back down later on and let him do a song with you so you can see what he got."

Wolf Man Jack said, "You ain't got to wait until later on, he could do something tonight if you want."

Sonny looked at me and asked, "So what'd you say Geney boy?"

I said bring it on, let's do it. I was so excited. I ain't been in Las Vegas for no time and all of a sudden, I'm about to get up on stage at a big hotel casino, The Bonanza. I was getting a chance to sing in front of the Las Vegas people for my first time and Sonny is gonna get a chance to see me do my thing. He was hoping I was good, but I knew beyond a shadow of a doubt wasn't anything gonna stop me now. I knew I was better than good, but I was getting the chance to prove myself.

So, we talked with Wolf Man and had a couple of drinks. When he went back up on stage he said, hey guys and gals, we got a young guy here by the name of Gene Anderson that heavyweight champion Sonny Liston brought in town from St. Louis. How about we give him a round of applause.

Man, people gave me a nice round of applause, but they was really applauding for Sonny. Sonny stood up as if he's going to sing and told me to get on up there and show them what you got. He was so proud of me man because I wasn't scared. I showed no fear. He didn't get like nothing that was chicken and nothing that was afraid of anything. I can hear him telling me to go get them Geney Boy, get them. I know you can do it, I know you can do it.

So, when I got up on the stage, the girls got to screaming because I had this beautiful outfit on man that they had never seen. People had been watching me just like I was a freak show at the Ringling Brothers Circus in his outfit. They had never seen an outfit like this, especially just a regular Black guy. They didn't know who I was. They knew I had to really be somebody because I was there with Sonny Liston. Back then they had never seen anything that looked like this because this was a new look that I dreamed up and had made.

When I hit the stage I told the band let's do a Wilson Pickett song, *In the Midnight Hour*. That was one of the songs I was crazy about at that time. The band hit it as if we had rehearsed it every night and when they hit it, I spun around with a triple spin, grabbed the mic and started stepping and singing. I hit the first note, and the people went absolutely crazy. Boy, I walked from one end of the stage to the other. I was holding the girls, kissing their hands, and singing and the band was jumping and moving.

Sonny was almost like he was in a big prize fight. He was up there hollering and dancing. Sonny can dance now. He was doing the Boogaloo, and the house was rocking. I mean we rocked that joint. I must have sung the song ten minutes and it ain't but a three-minute record. I must have done 14 courses of it, and they didn't even try to stop me. We just rocked it and rolled it man.

Wolf Man Jack was like, yeah guys and gals, I told you all. He was pumping it up and I felt so good. Man, I felt like I had conquered the world right then. I had to show my friend Sonny Liston that the time he was investing in me, and love he was showing me was not going to be wasted. I really did have something other than just a bunch of talk. Man, he was so excited he grabbed me when I got offstage and held my hand up like a heavyweight champion who had just won a big fight. Wolf Man Jack was trying to talk to him, and people was trying to talk to him, but Sonny had something else on his mind.

Boy, as soon as we got in the car there was a bunch of people crowding around wanting his autograph. He had to take time to sign autographs then he gave a guy $5 that chauffeured the car and took me straight over to the West Side where all stars used to go. We went to a club by the name of Silver Hill. On the way over there he was trying to explain to me what was going on. This club was owned by a guy named Bob Bailey, who was Pearl Bailey's brother or cousin or something like that. Anyway, Bob Bailey was a big politician on the west side of town, which was the Black side of town where the segregated line was drawn. Over on that side of town was a whole other world. It was glitzy and glamorous, but it wasn't like the Strip. They had small casinos and businesses but they're all Black owned. It was sort of like what I would have expected in any other city in the world other than Las Vegas. As far as I was concerned it was still like heaven to me. Back in those days, it was wide open and there was just as much activity going over there but it was on the Black hand side. I had already asked Sonny where are the Black people, where are our folks?

Finally, I arrived over there on the west side of town where I felt much more comfortable and I felt much more at home because I was surrounded by my familiar element. During those times a place called the Brown Derby at Moulin Rouge was the spot. I think Joe Lewis and Sammy Davis and all those stars got together and built it or something. It was the most premier place on the West Side. White stars like Milton Berle, Frank Sinatra, and Vic Demone all had black girlfriends. They would go over to these clubs and party with Black showgirls at the Moulin Rouge. They had straight Las Vegas Strip atmosphere over there with the brightly lit casinos, the huge showrooms, and the dancing girls. They had the same thing that you had up on the Strip. At the Moulin Rouge, Sonny walked in, and everybody went crazy.

Man, Sonny really got loose. He had never had a drink until we got to the Moulin Rouge. He took one sip of vodka, and he began to loosen up just a little bit more and a little bit more. He started dancing on the floor with the girls. He had two girls, one in front and one in back dancing with them. I'm having the time of my life, because I take it, this is how the game goes. I'm gonna do it like the big boys do it. Without thinking I'm dancing with a girl in front of me and a girl in the back of me. I'm partying like a dog then somewhere over on the side at the bar there was a bunch of Pimps.

I don't know why, but Sonny must have had a bad experience with them somewhere down the trail, so he told me to stay away from them guys, because they ain't nothing but trouble. The pimps knew Sonny because they would catch him drunk and vulnerable and sick the girls on him. They would clip Sonny sometimes and take things from him.

Sometimes Sonny would get mad and go through a lot of changes with them, so they really did have a pretty bad relationship. But Sonny knew how to deal with all of that and as far as I was concerned, I had been around that element time after time in my life, so I knew too.

This other side of life I was trying to adapt to was stardom. Sonny had lifted me to that level or was lifting me towards that level. I was learning but this street life, I was up on that part. I like slid over beside them because they was watching me. I was looking sort of like them, but I had stepped it up just a notch. I had a whole brand-new concept of this bell bottom. They were just graduating into my look that I had already been into. My element had come from that particular visual look, so we had something in common, these guys at the bar and myself.

They saw me with Sonny, so we started talking. The girls had him preoccupied but he was keeping an eye on me. Quiet as it was kept, I was going to keep an eye out because I could see that he was getting a little tipsy. He was slipping just a little bit. That Smirnoff vodka had Sonny loosening up just a little bit more and little bit more. I saw more and more of those girls circling him like vultures. He was having the time of his life, but he still was being cautious. I could tell he was feeling responsible for me. Before we know it, he's offered another way of life that really isn't for the heavyweight champion. He's back into the world of Game.

Game was something that Sonny really wasn't a master at because he didn't have patience for it. It really was too small for him because Sonny was a very serious person when the serious times was necessary. Sometimes as he got under the influence of alcohol it would stimulate that raw side of Sonny Liston. Some things that he used to feel were adventurous really were dangerous if you look at it in a sober-minded manner. I started seeing all this going on around Sonny you know. As I said, I wasn't very familiar with the stardom part but more the streetwise thing. I had grown up around a bunch of slick pimps, gangsters, dope pushers, and people like that.

Being an entertainer 95% of my life, I was out in the fast lane, but I was trying to get away from that element. I thought you eliminated that after you got to a certain level in entertainment, not knowing that they only became more and more affiliated with each other. As you begin to grow, you have to defend yourself from these elements or eliminate yourself from these elements by understanding them and recognizing them immediately when you see them and dismiss yourself from those circumstances.

I could tell that Sonny was more concerned about me being vulnerable in this situation than he was concerned about himself being in it. And I was more concerned about Sonny being consumed in this element, then I was worried about it being a problem for me. I knew how to handle myself in this type of game and so did Sonny, but we didn't know each other's weak points and strong points yet. We would learn each other, but the one thing that I did know is he legitimately did care about me and felt 100% responsible for me. I somehow felt the same about Sonny. In recognizing this, I knew I had to get us back on track for what we originally started out to do and that was go to Sugar Hill Club, where Bob Bailey had all of the stars hanging out every night. I wanted to be around some more stars, but not many stars were at the Moulin Rouge that particular night because it was like an off night. I didn't really like the environment because I had already been spoiled. I had been to the Tropicana, and I had been to the Bonanza. I hadn't seen all the other major hotels and casinos that we passed on the way to the west side that I want to investigate. Right now, I wanted to go to Sugar Hill where they had the best bands. Being a young entertainer as I was that time, all I wanted to do was just sing my ass off and let the whole Las Vegas know I'm here, and I come to take over.

So, I finally convinced Sonny lets go to Sugar Hill because I wanted him to really see me sing some more. You know, I wanted him to really get into what I was trying to do. And some old girl, I think her name was Candace or something, asked Sonny who I was and what I was doing here. Her whole intention was to try to get Sonny in there to trick him so they could steal the few hundreds he had in his pocket for that day as they had been doing on and off. I found out in the long run that Sonny told them who I was, his boy from St. Louis. He said, "He's the star and I'm going to take him over to Sugar Hill and he's going to sing over there. So, we can get together probably later on."

I looked at them like bitch, I will put my foot in your ass if you try to pull some slick shit on Sonny while I'm here. I really felt like I was hip to what was going on. It took a blind man not to see, but Sonny by that time got halfway tipsy. When he got halfway tipsy, I knew that those pimps up against the bar had to stick these broads on Sonny and it was something that they had been doing all the time. But they had been doing it without a guy like me around Sonny because everybody else was trying to use him for their benefit. Nobody I could see at that time was really trying to have Sonny's best interests at heart. All they would do is treat Sonny like a cash cow. When he gets over that, amongst that kind of vicious circle, he will become vulnerable and be open to anything they would bring to him. It didn't make a difference to him because he knew that little money that he was throwing away didn't mean that much to him at that time. He was handling a lot of money and when they cut him like that, they knew they could use them as a steppingstone. They could all make some money on him, so they was really just waiting in the same way they've cashed in on him over and over again.

This time it was different, and they could see it because as they knew I was a different kind of guy. They normally have seen him with some shady characters. White, Italian gangster guys or small-town mobsters hang out with him. They all have one thing on their mind to go get some girls, freak out with them, spend a little money and do some crazy shit. Sonny was always up for it because he would have so much time that he'd be confined to being a prize fighter. He could never let loose because he had to be in training, or he had to be under this supervision or that supervision. When he did let loose or had nothing scheduled, he was just like a beehive. He was full of energy and needed to do a lot of wild things because he was somehow trying to find something to take up the boredom in his life. Sonny stayed bored. He had a very brilliant mind and always wanted to be busy doing something. Nothing could occupy his time like fighting. He'd been in the gym, preparing for a fight and like it was the highlight of his life. He knew that would give him the attention and the love that he craved.

In time, Sonny revealed a lot of things to me. He revealed that his childhood was horrible, and his daddy was such a mean person to him. Life dealt him such a cruel deck of cards, and he was never able to get the love and affection that most kids got. Sonny never even owned a pair of shoes until he was well into his teens. He walked from Mississippi I think to St. Louis. He had never had no love in his life. It was always hard knocks and hard lessons.

All this stayed in his heart and in his mind, he never hardly discussed it until later on in life. As our association grew and we became more confident in one another, he began to express these things a lot more. This is why I can understand what motivated him to consistently veer off into some strange activities. People used to say this or that is wrong with Sonny. But it wasn't that there was something wrong with Sonny, this is how his response was. He was sensitive about how life had treated him. That's why being champ for such a little time was so precious to him. This is probably why he reached down to help me. He probably saw something of himself in me even at our first meeting at the gym. Something made him consistently stay up with me because there are a thousand reasons why Sonny could have just forgotten about me. Guys came to him every day trying to get signed because of his celebrity status. Apparently, he felt instinctively about me and him and a bonding friendship that was successful. In time he lived long enough to see that he was absolutely right.

Eventually he walks over to one of the girls that the pimps had been putting on him. This was a great big red bone stallion. I think her name was Sweet Pea or something like that. He said something in her ear, and she gave him the okay. He said, "Okay Gene baby, let's go over to Bob's joint." We get into the Cadillac and for the first time he pulls out a joint of weed. I said, champ smoking weed! I'm thinking, you know, I can't see him smoking weed. I can't see him doing none of that. Drinking was enough, but smoking weed?

I smoked weed every day during them days. I was a young weed head because I was a rock and roll, psychedelic musician. It was all cool with me, so we smoked a joint and rolled over toward Sugar Hill. I'm saying to myself, damn, I'm smoking weed with Sonny Liston man. Everything that seemed like the norm of an everyday person seemed like it was extremely exceptional because it was me and Sonny. We were doing this, and it was blowing my mind, but I was trying to act real cool like this is an everyday thing. But God knows it was no everyday thing, not even the thought of being in Las Vegas was an everyday thing.

But what was an everyday thing was the scene I had just left with all the players and stuff because I knew how to handle them guys. I've been handling them guys and putting them in their place for many years. As far as I was concerned, I was never going to try to get distracted up in that game because that game was always being forced upon me. I had no intention of being caught up in it because I was looking forward in my life, or what was happening right now with me and Sonny.

So, we finally went to Sugar Hill. It was a cozy little joint, but it was really modern and laid out and had a big garden in the back. Everybody stood back there and smoked their weed and stuff. When I walked in there was a whole bunch of stars in there. Kyle Stacy was hanging out and Lou Rawls was up in there. A bunch of stars like that was hanging out and they had white girls. Black guys and white girls and a bunch big time pimps up in there. Some of the old pit bosses, some old mobsters from the Bugsy Siegel days, old guys got young showgirls up in there.

It was going on. The band was bumping. I think he was Huck Daniels and them and their Soul Patrol. Some of those guys was like a walking jukebox. They could play every song that you've ever heard on the radio and played better than the radio. When I come in the door with Sonny everybody started hollering Sonny boy, Sonny boy!

One reason they used to be like that about Sonny other than they did like him, Sonny spent a lot of money and had big tabs. Most of the time they knew they would make a quota if Sonny is in there. Sonny spent $3,000 in a joint if he really felt good about being there, because he was handling money at that time, more than just the average guy. He had still been heavyweight champion of the world, and they owed him a lot of money. He knew they owed him that phantom Fight Money sometime down the trail and was going to have to pay up. He discussed it with me on and off, little by little. I never got into that until way later into our relationship. I asked him why he spent so much money, and he would tell me it looked like a lot of money on my level, but on his level, it ain't nothing but crumbs.

Then all of a sudden there he was, Mr. Bob Bailey. He's a tall black guy, real wavy hair, extremely immaculately dressed and spoke with a very educated accent. Everybody loved him because Bob was the ultimate of all-time players. Bob had built this joint. This place was the Mecca for all of the real in crowd, hip guys on both sides of the strip. The big-time guys and the big-time players over on the West Side would all come to Bob Bailey's joint and hang out. If you wanted to catch a halfway rich White girl, you might even get Phyllis Diller up in there. You might catch Debbie Reynolds or somebody, you never know who's gonna come up in Bob's joint.

Them pimps was known for knocking off some big name, White celebrity broads up in there. They would go over there because they have a hunger to try to get with some Black dudes. To keep it on the low-low QT they would come to the Bob Bailey joint cause they know that all the look-a-loos wouldn't be over there in your business. Bob Bailey didn't have that. It was an exclusive club for just players and celebrities and those that really wanted to be incognito to do their own thing with no apprehension. Bob made it safe for those types of people to be there. He had bodyguards walking them to their cars and security guards to watch the cars.

Oh man, he would give long tabs. Bob was a real player and politician. I didn't know but Bob probably had the drugs and everything. Whatever it was, they'd be outside on the patio, smoking weed, tooting cocaine, and popping champagne. It was a lively atmosphere, and Bob would stay open till the sun came up. Bob would stay open until five, six and seven o'clock in the morning and the place would still be packed.

In Las Vegas back then the air conditioning system wasn't massively out there. It was just in major casinos and so people would have to go home when the sun rose. Then the nights was the days, and the days was the nights so we would party. We partied in Bob's joint until we couldn't party no more. I'm a country boy so I don't know about this. I'm yawning and sleepy, but I'm still trying to stay up with Sonny and keep on rolling.

Sonny goes to Bob and introduces me to him. "Hey, Bob, this is my boy Geney Boy from St. Louis. This boy is one of the greatest entertainers I've seen in years. I had him fly out here to be with me. I want you to put him on the stage with that band you got there, and I want to let him rock the house for you. Is that okay?"

Bob said, "Yes Sonny boy, anything you want. What have you ever done?"

I told him who I was, what I've done, blah, blah, blah. I lied a little bit.

Bob said, "Well, hey, let me see you doing something." Then he called the bandleader down and he whispered something in his ear. "This is Sonny boy's boy. In other words, take care of him. Let him do a number or two and let's see what he's working with."

Dude said, "Okay, man, what's your name?"

I told him my name is Gene Anderson.

He asked what I wanted to do. I said I want to do something funky — something like *Papa's Got a Brand-New Bag* and *Knock on Wood* back-to-back. "Man, it's some funky songs and listen, if you can't play it, get out the kitchen if it's too hot for you."

He looked at me and busted out laughing. "Boy, you got heart. Come on up here." He got up to the mic and introduced me. He said, "Ladies and Gents, we got a guy here that the champ brought in. Sonny Liston, stand up boy and take a bow."

Sonny stood up like he usually does. But this time he's a little drunk and he's stumbling over tables and shit. He raised his hand up like a champion is supposed to. He said, "Come on Geney boy!"

I throw kisses to the crowd. When I showed up, they saw the cape, and the alligator stuff all over me. They had never seen it before. I'm looking like a spaceman to these people. I know I'm just extremely different because that was my style. So, I slowly walked up to the microphone, and I looked at the people as if David is going to conquer Goliath. I had all the confidence in the world man because I was still hopped up over the fact that I'm in Las Vegas. I had already wiped out one joint, Moulin Rouge, and I already had competition with all the pimps of the players over there. Back in those days Las Vegas was absolutely a very small community, and they will say that Sonny has a young player from St. Louis, and they was over here on the West Side.

As I looked around, I could see the tension in the room. Everybody was waiting for the first note because they knew Sonny had never come over there and tried to do anything but party. He had never brought anybody over there as an artist or entertainer to represent and this was like let's see what he's got. Come on boy let's see what you working with. So, I turned around to the band. James Brown couldn't have done it no better boy. I did this one leg James Brown spin. Man, the people was up on the tables rocking the joint.

Sonny was screaming and hollering just like a Girl Scout. He was hollering, "Come on Geney Boy, come on." Bob Bailey was bobbing his head like yeah, man, we found one. Man, I was dancing and was doing splits. Man, let me tell you. I felt like I was on top of the world. Like James Cagne said, "Look ma I'm on top of the world." Well, I felt the same way. *Look, ma, I'm on top of the world.* In my mind, I could see that this might be my turning point, or I can get the chance to see Sammy now and get to rolling. Everything was going to work itself out.

Sonny almost came on stage and got me, man. He was so proud of me and the people just patting me on the back and everything. I was excited because, you know, all this was brand new to me. This was like my dream coming true. Sonny took me right over to Bob and say, "Hey, Bob didn't I tell you my kid had it?"

Bob said, "Yeah, man. Listen, you know I got a TV show. Bring him down next week and let's see if we can get him on and pump him up, man. Yeah, we can book him right here in our club."

Sonny said, "Well okay baby boy, let's roll."

Then walking through the door here she comes — the big yellow gal. She followed him all the way from the Moulin Rouge over to Bob Bailey's Sugar Hill. He spots her and tells her to come over here. "Geney boy, look who's here." There she was with two other young girls with her, all of them looking like French whores. Man, they had the shortest skirts. The wigs was long, and all kinked up because they've been out hustling all night. The word had been out all over the West Side that Sonny Liston is out, and he's drunk and partying. That was nothing but a green light for all the hoes to track him down.

I didn't know but in time I found out this had been a ritual. They knew if they could find him, he was going to really spend some money. He's going to trick with everybody that he could until he ran out of money, ran out of time, or ran out of fresh whores because he didn't like to do the same girl twice especially in one night. So, he had to have more than one, and they had to be very different and unique in their own way. This is what the big yellow gal knew. Guess that's why she was acting sort of like a madam. She brought these other two girls with her so they could trick with him all night long, working for the few hundred dollars that he had left. They used to dig when he was running loose, partying over there on the West Side. Little did I know that this would be a brand-new experience. It will be my first orgy with those three whores — Sonny Liston and me.

Golden Nights

Sonny spotted the big yellow girl. She comes in there with two other broads who looked like they've been whoring all night. But they was sexy looking to me. I said, "man, look at these sexy, pretty Black gals."

This was a new thing for me because I knew a lot of hoes, but I never had an encounter where they were gonna pursue me, as these ones were. I'm sure the big yellow girl had told them that Sonny got a new guy with him that he listens to. We gotta get past him to get to Sonny. So, they started to work on me. They started asking people how I sounded, because they missed the show. They wanted me to get out there and sing again. I was just trying to show off I guess because I was young, and I was trying to meet people. There's no better way than a bunch of hoes talking about you up and down the track.

There was one girl about my height, brown-skin girl, built like a brick house, Mary Anne. Just as spicy and flirty as she could be and she was rubbing up on me. Sonny started looking at me and laughing because he knew I was just a little bit uncomfortable. The truth about the issue was I was married. I never done anything really bad to my marriage. I felt that marriage is a sacred thing. I knew there was a lot of women who liked me because I was a star. I was out in the public and my job was to make them like me, but I had never cheated on my wife. A lot of people may have thought I cheated, but it was just an act. Some of my young, beautiful female fans thought that they could get the chance to get a hold of me or get up with me. I mean you just flirt with them and lead them on.

But in the end, you just go back home to your wife and be a family man. I had that in me, that amount of discipline about myself, but this was different. I was in a foreign area. I was with Sonny Liston. I guess the devil got me. I'm being enticed by this young beautiful girl named Mary Anne, and she's rubbing up on me, and playing with my dick. I'm saying, "Ah man, I can't do this here, I got a wife." But Sonny was so excited because he didn't like no sissy-like boys, you know, he liked real macho guys. Up to this point I've shown I was an absolutely strong-hearted, macho, hard-core brother. He just knew this is what I want to do, because people have a tendency to think that you think like them. Especially when you're their guest and they're trying to show you their hospitality.

Now that's where it really was with Sonny if I'm being truthful. He really wasn't trying to disrespect my marriage or entice me into doing things that weren't my norm. This is just how he thought. Sonny was a real open party guy. When he had time available to do this it was just one of the ways he'd show his love for me. He THOUGHT this was what I probably wanted and wasn't able to do. He was gonna show me how to do things on a rock star level or a big baller, Las Vegas style.

Sonny was a part of that old era of mafia gangster guys. Back in those days in Las Vegas there was three things, booze, broads, and drugs. Sonny was really just being normal at what he does especially if he was drunk and partying out of control. They knew this. They had been trying to get him over on the West Side for some time, but Sonny was busy doing different things, big things like he had big fights coming up. It was hard to have him break his training regimen and to get over there amongst them and do certain things. They were missing the money to be truthful because Sonny was spending money like it was no tomorrow when he was on one of these binges.

So, we partied and fraternized, carried on as wild as you could possibly imagine, for quite a while. The sun looked like it was about to come up, then Sonny suggested that we all should go to the hotel, over to the Stardust on the strip. Now the Stardust, I had no idea, was Sonny's headquarters. That was basically where he hung out and had his biggest juice. The mob boys who signed him actually, after he won the championship with Floyd Patterson, had their headquarters at the Stardust. Guys like Yale Cohen, Ash Resnick, and even Morris Shenker and them (the guys that St. Louis mob that own the Dunes Hotel at the time) used to hang out over there. Matter of fact, all the Kansas City mobs guys, the St. Louis mob guys, and some of the guys from back east, frequented the Stardust because it seemed to be neutral territory, where everybody felt at home.

Sonny gave me the keys. I'm feeling like, oh baby boy this gotta be a movie or something. I'm driving a brand-new Cadillac, not the old hoopty I was driving back in St. Louis. Sonny is in the back seat, with two girls just rubbing on him and feeling his dick, kissing on him, and probably sticking their hand in his pocket. And I got Mary Anne in front with me and she just kissing on me, and I can hardly drive. She damn near on the dashboard showing me her pussy, and sticking my finger in her pussy, and drinking that vodka, and smoking that weed. It was a wild situation. I'd never experienced nothing like this before and it was getting out of hand for me, but I wasn't trying to punk out. I was trying to act like this was an everyday thing for me too, (as far as they was concerned).

Sonny was looking every now and then and pushing back off them, to make sure that I was okay. "Geney boy, Geney boy, is you alright?"

I would say "Yeah Sonny boy, I'm in heaven baby."

He'd say "Ahh that's what I'm talking about, I just want you to feel good. We gonna party all day, baby! Aint that right?!"

I say, "Yeah Sonny boy, we gonna party 'til we can't no more."

He bust out with that big affectionate laugh, "I told you Geney boy is alright. Geney boy's down with me." So, after a few wrong turns not knowing where I was going, I got instructions from Mary Anne, and we finally made it to the Stardust on the strip.

Man, it was like so many bright lights in front of the building. They had a great big, huge sign with a lot of different color stars sparkling and the sign read Stardust Hotel. Man, it was electrifying. It was twilight and they was acting like it was twelve noon. It was just too much comprehend for a young country boy, who'd never seen anything like this much excitement. It was the rich guys with the limousines and the broads with the long mink coats on. In those days you had to be very flashy and dressed up, you couldn't be as casual as you are today in Las Vegas. You had to be top notch in those times.

And when we pulled up to the front, the parking attendant jumped straight to the door and opened it as we slowly got out the car. Everybody seemed to freeze when they saw him. By this time, he was a different Sonny Liston than the one that picked me up at the airport. His shirt was all lip sticked up, smelling like Smirnoff vodka, and he was just as wild and loose as they come. But he was cheerful and still happy, laughing real loud. A lot of the sophisticated people were looking at him like, "I told you he was a heathen." But all the old playas and gangstas was like, "Oh yeah that's Sonny boy, that's the Sonny boy we know."

I was trying to digest everything that was going on around me. At the same time, I was trying to look out for Sonny because I didn't know this was the norm when he would go on these binges. I was being totally distracted by Mary Anne. She was holding on to me for dear life, especially when we got in front of all these lights because she didn't really know who I was. But she thought I was about as big as Rick James or James Brown or somebody, because I was with Sonny. She was trying to get into the spotlight. People was taking pictures like you wouldn't believe, because that was still Sonny Liston. I was right there with him, and they didn't know who I was, but I was flashy. I got all these girls with me, all this buzz is going around us, so they was takin' pictures. She was up under me trying to get her little fifteen minutes of fame too.

So, we walked through the door, and in the lounge was a band, Johnny Rico, doing stuff like Bobby Darin and the Four Freshman, real pop stuff (it was going on big at the time). Sonny went over and sat down at the table and knocked over glasses of water. He was drunk as a skunk, but people knew Sonny. I'm kind a like embarrassed but hell, that was Sonny. He can do what he want to do, I'm just with him, that's all. So somewhere in there they got his order, the Smirnoff vodka and everybody had a round.

Then he tells me, "Go to the front desk and ask for a guy by the name of Yale Cohen." Yale Cohen was one of the big bosses over there at the Stardust that had been put in the position by the mob. Yale was a guy that Sonny always got in touch with when he needed some money. Yale would always take Sonny's marker and was always cool. Some of those guys, honest to God truly did love Sonny Liston. All the mob guys loved him, because Sonny had done a lot of things with them. As time went by, he started to reveal some of the intimate things he had been affiliated with, some capers I sometimes cringe at the thought of. If I was in his position, would I have the heart to have done it, or been a part of it? But they knew Sonny. "Sonny's a good boy, he's one of us."

So, I went up to the counter and asked for Yale Cohen. He comes out and I can't even remember exactly what he looked like. All I know is he was a tough looking old guy. He said, "Yeah, cat."

I said, "Sonny boy want to see you."

He said, "Where that son of a bitch at?"

I say, "He over there in the lounge looking at the Johnny Rico show."

He said, "Come on, let's go." We walked over to the lounge. Everybody was looking when Mr. Cohen walked by. All the dealers and the small paper bosses were saluting like he was General MacArthur. He was walking with me and talking, "Aye kid, I ain't seen you around here before."

I say, "Yeah, I ain't from around here. I'm from St. Louis."

"Oh, you from Morris Shenker's town."

I say, "I know who Morris Shenker is." (Because he had a large law office, he would get all the big boys out the jail and out from behind bars in St. Louis. In the world of politicians, they all knew who Morris Shenker was.)

Then he asked me, "What you doing out here young fella? Ain't you a long way from home?"

I told him, "Yeah, I came out here to be with Sonny. He gonna introduce me to Sammy Davis Jr., the entertainer. Maybe I can get my career kick started and be a big star in Las Vegas like the rest of these guys."

"Well, you sure got the heart for it, if you are hanging around here with guys like Sonny." He started laughing real hard. He said, "Well, come on." Then he put his arm around me and started walking. Man, it seemed like it was a million-mile walk, with his big ole' pistol bumping up against my side. In those days all the big boys and bosses had thirty-eights hanging out their pockets or in shoulder holsters. They kept their guns with them all the time back then, the olden days like. Because his gun was against me, my heat started beating like man, this is really the mob for real, I'm really caught up in stuff.

I was like in one breath "Yeah, this is the real thing," and in the other breath it was, "Oh shit what have I got myself into?" But whatever it is, I know I'm gonna be okay because I was still with Sonny Liston. At the time I felt like nothing could be stronger because I was his boy, his true boy. In my heart I was trying to be his true friend. In time, in his actions and in his eyes, I knew that he felt the same way about me, that he was gonna be a true friend to me.

So, when we got over there where Sonny was, Sonny saw him, "Oh yeah, Cohen baby." Him and Sonny hugged like two old schoolgirls, like they hadn't seen each other in God knows how many years. They saw each other that week sometime. Anyway, Sonny whispered in his ear, and he looked at Sonny and threw his hands in the air. Then Sonny whispered again, told him to bend down and whispered in his ear again.

There is a frustrating yet loving look on his face. He tells Sonny, "Have the kid walk over to the counter with me". So, I got up, and we walked up to the counter. On the way over there he says, "Listen kid, whatever you do, look out for Sonny boy, cause right now he aint in his right frame of mind, and he needs somebody like you around. I can tell you're a good kid." Right then and there, even though he was the mob, I can tell he really did like and care about Sonny.

So he had me wait outside his office, and in a few minutes, he came out with an envelope and a key. He handed them to me and instead of walking with them in my hand, I stuck them in my shirt. I didn't want to take a chance at losing whatever is in that envelope and that key. I stuck it in my shirt, and my pants were tucked in real tight. I hurried right over where Sonny was and he was dancing in the middle of the floor with all three of the girls, knocking stuff over. and people was laughing at him. Some of them was kind of upset and the pimp bosses said, "Yeah, he's on another one."

So, I got on the dance floor and boogalood my way to where he was. He saw me and his face lit up. He must have known it was okay because he began to dance a little wilder like James Brown. He pulled one pant leg up. Boy he was so funny with his big ole ass trying to do the James Brown. I started laughing and everyone's laughing. Before you knew it was a party going on at the Johnny Rico show on the dance floor. Shortly after that the band stopped and we walked over to the table.

I showed him the key and envelope. He said "Geney boy, hold that envelope real tight. Put it back in your shirt and let's go to the room." We walked through the lobby towards the elevators and Sonny stopped to sign a few autographs, and a few fans took a couple pictures. As tore up as he was, he was still doing the PR as a champion would. We finally got on the elevator, with some young couple. Sonny got to teasing the guy.

He said, "Hey man, what y'all on a honeymoon or something?"

The guy said, "Yeah, Mr. Liston. We on a honeymoon."

Sonny said plain and blatant, "You better fuck her real good tonight, if not she can come upstairs and I can fuck her good," then he started busting out laughing. The guy bust out laughing.

When they finally got off the elevator I said to myself "Sonny sho got some nerve." We busted out laughing and before you knew it, we had finally reached our floor. WHAT? THE PENTHOUSE! All the way to the top floor. When we got off the elevator you had to use a special key to get in. I couldn't figure out what the key was for. Man, I was like this must've been a presidential suite. He really was showing out for me this time. It had huge, big rooms. The rooms were so large if you was a skateboarder, you could've skateboarded and never ran into the furniture. The view was breathtaking. You could see all up and down the strip. You could see the cars, the people, the hotels, palm trees, and all of this felt like a dream. I'd never seen this before, only in movies, and not too many of those.

Then he walked up behind me and tapped my shoulder. It startled me because I was so engrossed in the view. I say, "Aye Sonny boy, this is something man." He said, "How you like it kid?"

"It's a dream come true."

"Son it's okay, but right now, get yo clothes off and let's go fuck these bitches."

When he said that I was like, "Here we go y'all, let's do it." But I had to tell him. "Hey, Sonny, what about the envelope?"

He said "Aye Geney boy, take care of that. Put it up somewhere safe, okay?" I knew what was on his mind because sooner or later them hoes were gonna try something slick like trying to steal some money from him. But he knew that this time it was gonna be different cause I had the money. He believed that I really was a responsible person and had his best interest at heart. So, I checked around and when no one was looking, I stuffed the envelope at the bottom of the curtain, where they had weights holding them down. I knew the money was safe, so now let the party begin.

I went into the restroom. There was a big, huge room surrounded by mirrors with a white shag rug. It had three different sections. One section where the toilet was, one section where the shower was, and a big – huge, damn near looked like a swimming pool – Jacuzzi. He and all three of the girls were in the Jacuzzi, and bubbles was everywhere.

I'd never seen anything like this before except in movies. But here I was, a country boy from St. Louis. All I could think was man what a world that I've been missing all of my life. Now I'm on the road of being a part of all the great things thanks to Sonny Liston. As I stood there this other girl began to walk up the steps of the Jacuzzi, one slow step at a time. The suds began to fall off her, and there she was built like a Black Greek Goddess, titties standing straight up. I didn't know at the time girls was having boob jobs. I thought she just had straight, hard point, beautiful titties and her body was built like an hourglass. She started walking towards me, and I'm damn near with my mouth open in a trance.

Then she slowly took my shirt off, then she unbuttoned my pants, they fell down to my ankles. She slowly pulled down my cotton drawls little by little and went down and took my left and right feet out of my clothes. Then she bent down and started licking me down my stomach. I started trembling somewhat, but I didn't want to show that I was nervous. I wanted Sonny to think this was an everyday thing. In my heart I knew it was something I had never experienced. In the back of my mind I kept thinking, "YOU'RE MARRIED GENE, YOU'RE MARRIED!" But what could I do? I was a victim of pressure at the moment. There was beautiful titties on this beautiful young girl. Dick was hard like it's about to break.

I closed my eyes, and that's when she gave me head. She must've been an extreme expert, cause I ain't that small of a guy. She swallowed the whole dick, all the way to the balls and all. My eyes rolled to the back of my head, like son of a bitch you talk about deep throat, she was a deep throat. After hitting three or four times I was up and running.

We both dived into the Jacuzzi, Sonny laughing his ass off. He talking about, "Geney baby whatcha think? We gone fuck these bitches or what?" He busted out with that big affectionate laugh, then Sweet Pea splashed her way over to me [and] Mary Anne. I began to suck on her titties and her eyes rolled back. The other girl began to kiss Mary Anne in the mouth. They was just sucking and petting on each other. Sonny had his hands in both girls' pussies. It was just like he was carrying two boxing gloves, he had hands full of pussy, after a while of playing and splashing around, we all got out of the Jacuzzi.

Got into the biggest king size-super king size bed I'd ever seen. It had poles and drapes on it. He was playing his favorite song, James Brown's *Night Train, (All aboard the night train),* from a cassette tape in his pocket. I remember it because it must've been on repeat. It played over and over, all night and day.

Them bitches were acting a fool. They was sucking pussy, one behind the other, they called it a daisy chain. Me and Sonny was doing a lot of laughing at them, we was getting a little bit in here and there. Then one girl started screaming, "Sonny no, Sonny no!" I looked around and Sonny had a dick the size of a baseball bat. She was steady hollering, "I can't take that, don't put it all in my mouth."

He said, "Bitch, if you can't put it inside your mouth, lick around this mothafucka, but you betta do something." Boy I just fell out laughing because that was just Sonny's personality. Sweet Pea and another girl got together, and they was giving him a blow job, an ass job, and he was screaming, "NIGHT TRAIN! NIGHT TRAIN! Geney boy, you like this?"

I was too busy trying to hump and pump on top of Mary Anne. She was just doing some things like hollering and moaning and shit. Then she grabbed my hand and stuck my finger in her ass. This was all strange and foreign to me, I'd never experienced anything this wild. After all, I was still a young country boy from St. Louis. I couldn't believe this was actually happening. Sonny was laughing because he saw on my face how uncomfortable I was with the whole scene. I was young doing what I thought I knew to do. Then Sonny whispered into Sweet Pea's ear and all of a sudden, she got off of him and crawled over to where I was. She started licking me all up and down my legs and back while this other girl was sucking my dick, like all over everywhere, like tickling me. I was trying to keep my composure. I was about to fall apart to tell the truth, but I was hanging in there like a real veteran. It was my very first time for something that radical.

Then Sonny decided to take the other pretty girl, with the long pretty titties. He threw her down and got ready to stick his dick in her, and she started screaming and hollering. He tried to push and push and couldn't get it in her. Sonny had a big horse dick, the girl was hollering she couldn't take it. He said "Geney baby, come over here and fuck this bitch so I can get my dick in this bitch." Now that was really a new one to me. Mary Anne and Sweet Pea bust out laughing because they knew what the deal was, but this was the young girl's first time with Sonny. Shit I was young, wild and loose by then, so I dived up on her and fucked and pumped her, and skidded up on her, all up on her face and everything. By then I had turned into a young wild fuck machine. By the time I skidded in her and got her all wet, Sonny said "Okay, okay, my turn."

He rushed his dick up in that bitch, but she hollered and screamed until she passed out. She literally fainted. Sweet Pea ran to the toilet and got a cold towel, put it on her forehead and face and she finally came to. He fucked this bitch totally unconscious. Then he called Mary Anne and said, "Come here, bitch,". You know Sonny was drunk. He drank two bottles of Smirnoff vodka. He done got real doggish and started to order them around and tell them to do this and that. Then Mary Anne got up and started putting on her clothes and her drawls. Then Sonny said, "Big ole bitch, where you going?"

She said, "Sonny, you didn't give that much money for us to have to go through this. I'm going unless you give us some more money. Cause we did everything that you wanted us to do."

He said, "Bitch, you aint going nowhere."

"Watch me." She started to pack her stuff.

He said "Geney baby, stop this bitch." Then he got very belligerent. "Grab this bitch and throw this bitch over the motherfucking balcony."

Throw her over the balcony? I'm saying to myself, what the fuck? All this partying, all this fun, then all of a sudden, it done turned ugly. What's going on? The other two girls saw that Sonny drank too much and damn near turned into a beast. They were familiar because they knew Sonny and had been to this point before with them and some more hoes. They knew the best thing was to get out of there as fast as they could, with all the money they could get from Sonny. They could just sneak out the door on him, anything to get away from him at this point. All I knew was that Sonny was upset, and he told me to do something I had never dreamed would happen.

Then he said it again, "Grab this bitch and throw this bitch over the motherfucking balcony." I looked in his face and seen the seriousness. Now I have a choice to make. Do something radical and crazy like this that's gonna get me into a lot of trouble, or just punk out and be like hey man and get on the hoes side? I don't know what to do but I know one thing, Sonny had decided to throw this bitch over the balcony. I think maybe I can grab this bitch and fake like I'm gonna throw her off the balcony and talk some sense into him before he grabs her and does it himself.

At that point the whole thing is gonna go down the drain. I won't get a chance to meet Sammy, I won't get a chance to get my dream together and be a star. Tomorrow he will wake up sober and he won't remember none of this. My wife will find out about it, my mom will find out about it, it will be all over the news. It's Sonny Liston, the ex-heavyweight champion of the world and everybody knows everything that he does. Sometimes when he's drunk like this, he does some crazy things. All I know is to make a quick decision, right now. What should I do?

So, I took plan B, fake like I was gonna throw this bitch over the balcony. I grabbed her by the neck and by the arm and twisted her up and started heading towards the balcony. I snatched open the doors, then the hoes got to hollering, "Please don't throw her out."

He said "Geney baby! Geney baby! Stop man! Stop man!" That's what I was hoping would happen. The Lord must've answered my silent prayer. He looked at me like this boy must be a fool or crazy or something. Mary Anne must've thought, 'I don't know where Sonny got him from, but we just finished fuckin' and suckin' and everything else, now he's gonna throw me over the balcony?' This guy gotta be crazy. Then I put her down.

All of a sudden there was a chill over the room. Everybody was looking at me all together in different ways, different than when they first came into the room. I was just a nice little happy go lucky guy, but then they saw the viciousness in me when I pretended I was gonna throw her off the balcony, because Sonny had said it. Sonny knew that we'd taken the party too far and tried to cool the situation. There's no telling what them hoes might've done. They may have gone to the police, which I doubt, or to their pimps and started a bunch of stuff, or the newspapers. Sonny was just that controversial of a person. They could've switched the story around in all kinds of ways, so he was trying to diffuse this thing that he caused.

So, he called me over to him and whispered in my ear, "Geney baby, go get that envelope that I told you to put up for me." So, I looked around making sure no one was watching where I stashed it and went to the curtains and pulled out the envelope. I sneaked it into his hand behind his back, so they couldn't see what's going on. He went into the envelope and pulled out a few bills and gave them all another hundred dollars each. He gave these hoes a hundred a piece, which was a lot of money back in them days. As far as I was concerned it was a lot of money period. I hadn't seen that many hundred-dollar bills given to no hoes no matter where I had been in my life, at that time. I felt like they was taking advantage of the moment and using Sonny straight through me, and I didn't like it even though we had gone a little too far.

Sonny said, "Geney baby, I want you to take these girls back over to the West Side and drop 'em off."

They said, "no, we gonna catch a cab."

He said, "No, Geney baby, you take 'em." They argued back and forth and decided to let me take them back to the West Side. They was very apprehensive of me, because I wasn't drunk like Sonny and I threatened to throw this girl off the balcony. They didn't know where I might come from. They were really right, because in my heart I was upset that they took that extra money from Sonny. He had already given them two or three hundred a piece anyway, way too much money. Them was cheap hoes, they wasn't worth more than twenty to twenty-five dollars, period. He done overpaid them and they didn't really treat him too right all the time.

In the end, everybody got dressed, and I took the hoes out the door. We went through the lobby and people were still looking at me like that's the guy who was with Sonny, that's the youngster that was with Sonny. Is that Sonny's son? They was still looking at this crazy looking outfit I got on and thought I must've been a pimp or something because they knew these were hoes. They was kinda holding on to me, and I knew that they had been screaming, trying to get out of the hotel with that money. They knew they had played Sonny once again, and I didn't really like it. So, we got into the car and started heading to the West Side.

I didn't say too much but they was just kept talking to me, trying to figure out where I was coming from and who I was to Sonny. They asked a lot of personal questions. So, we got there to Bonanza Street, close to the Moulin Rouge. I was getting furious, boiling inside because I'm listening to these hoes saying how they played Sonny and how they gonna do it next time, as if I wasn't even there. They knew that I wasn't to be played with, I could tell by the way they was kind of being timid talking to me. Something said, jack these hoes up, don't let them do Sonny like that. So, I pulled over to the curb, got out of the car and snatched the car door open. I said, "You hoes break yourself."

Them hoes looked at me as if they was surprised I said it like that. I said, "You heard me right hoes, break yourself." I grabbed Sweet Pea, the big yellow one. I grabbed her because I knew she was the boss. I grabbed her and shook that bitch, "Break yourself bitch." She went in her pocketbook and pulled out a couple hundreds, and the other girls I told to break theyself. Then I thought this was robbery. I said, "I don't believe you did Sonny right so I'm gonna take half of this money."

Them hoes was so fucking nervous cause I'm sure they remember I was about to throw one of them hoes up off the balcony. I didn't have no fear on my face, and I was serious about what I said. They hurried up and gave me that money with a quickness. I slammed the door and walked back around the car, cape flying in the air like one of them pimps of the superfly days. So, I asked them hoes, "Where do you want me to drop y'all off at?" I was talking real crazy and tough.

One thing I was really sleepy because I wasn't used to being up no day and a half or two days like that. I was really irritable cause I'm thinking I'm into some shit that I really didn't want to be a part of. It was cool for a minute, but now I done turned ugly and got into pimp mode. I don't want to be no pimp, I'm interested in trying to be a star. The situation called for me to do what's necessary and that's what I was doing. I knew one thing, if I didn't push them hoes in a corner and jack them up for that money, I might as well put a dress on myself because I wasn't Sonny. Sonny was known to be vulnerable in those types of situations because he was a big celebrity caught up in small time shit. Because of his habits of running loose, free, phreaking' with all of them hoes, they was used to taking advantage of him. The pimps used to set him up. I didn't want to be known as that type of vulnerable person, knowing that I was gonna be with Sonny longer than I had anticipated. They thought that I was just a guy for the moment, but I was gonna be there all day every day. I knew he wasn't gonna change his activities and the way he conducted himself. I had to be a real true friend to him if it took the hard side of the hard or the soft side of the road.

I believed in my heart, Sonny had the power, money, juice, and the desire to get me out of any situation I got into where I was trying to protect his interest. Sonny had that kind of credibility with me, because that was really the kind of guy Sonny was. The mob only believes in honor among thieves. Me and Sonny, in my heart was gonna become as thick as thieves. So, I asked them hoes where they want to go because I was for putting them hoes out right there by the Moulin Rouge. They said they want to go to a place called Reuben's. Reuben's was a place where all the pimps, hoes, hustlers, number backers, and all those types of people would get together before the sun came up.

The sun was running 110 to 125 and air conditioning wasn't that plentiful back in those days. So, everybody would stay out all night, sleep all day then get out early the next night then pimp some more. That was their everyday routine. They showed me what street to get on. I forgot what street it was now, but when I pulled up in front of Reuben's it was lined up back-to-back with Cadillacs, Lincolns, Mercedes, all chopped up with the Superfly look. That look existed long before the motion picture came out. So, I knew this had to be where all the hardcore playas hung out.

I was accustomed to seeing that type of environment. Before I went out there with Sonny, I had been an entertainer in Chicago, Detroit, and Memphis so I knew that scene. I jumped out of the car, and everybody that was hanging outside the joint was looking at me like wassup with this? They see Mary Anne, they see Sweet Pea, they know that it was Sonny Liston's car, but they had never seen me before. I'm all G'd out with this new outfit on, they are looking at me like where did this guy come from. He got Sonny's car and got these known hoes. Is this a new pimp on the set or what? I'm looking at them hoes, snapping my fingers like clocks switching because they knew I wasn't to be played with. These hoes already done tested me and I done passed the test, jacked 'em up, threatened them hoes up, and I'm still smooth about it.

So, the first thing them hoes do is take me straight to Mr. Reuben. I'm kind of apprehensive because I know I ain't discover these hoes, they belong to somebody. These ain't just straight renegade hoes out here, these hoes out for money. There was a band playing in Reuben's. The band was funky, and I knew something about music. I kinda eased over to the band but Mr. Reuben was watching me. Everyone was kinda watching me. Them hoes stayed even though I had stuck 'em up. They kept moving with me and started buying drinks, acting like I really was their pimp.

I'm sitting here like damn, what kind of dumb ass bitches is these? I done kicked 'em in their ass, took all of their fucking money, I done fucked 'em and everything else. I'm trying see if I can sneak out with some type of credibility and get the fuck away from there and back to

Sonny. But I want to see this band now, and these hoes is steady putting me on front street as if they done chose a nigga.

All of sudden Mr. Reuben walks over to me and says, "Hey man. I have never seen you around her before. They tell me you got Sonny's car. Where's Sonny boy at?"

Everybody always knew if they saw Sonny boy he was gonna spend some money. Reuben knows when the pimps brought the hoes, they wouldn't spend no money in his place. But he did like Sonny, come to find. I knew I had to smooth it out with Mr. Reuben some kinda way because he had a band in this place and I thought it might be a good joint to get started in. I'd have Sonny bring me over there later on so I could sit in with the band. In the meantime, we started discussing my purpose for being in Las Vegas, and who I was. He found out that I was an entertainer, and some of the people I worked he knew so he asked me if I wanted to sit in with the band.

Now that was a whole other twist. From a bad situation with the hoes and Sonny, all the arguing and fighting, to sticking them hoes up, back to singing and dancing again. Boy this roller coaster that I'm on right now, no telling where the twist and turns gonna take me. So, I told him to let me talk to the band and see what they know. Maybe I can do a number before I go back and pick up Sonny.

He had called the band leader down to talk to me. We sat down and chatted for a moment, then I noticed out the side of my eye the other hoe (can't think of her name) was up against the bar with some dude. He had to be a pimp by the way he was dressed at the time. Apparently, she was telling him what went down on the date with Sonny, why her money was looking funny. I saw him gawking at me looking back at the hoe, and I knew that the conversation was concerning the issues that had gone down. But I knew the code to pimpin' was that if she put herself in that position, she supposed to get broke. Those were the rules, and I was familiar with them because I've been around it so much, but I really wasn't trying to make a career. My career was singing and dancing and trying to be a star. Life has a tendency to take you where it wants you to go, more so than where you try to direct yourself. Everybody assumed that's what my vocation was.

Now I'm sitting down talking to Mr. Reuben about entertainment. But his real purpose is to try to warm up to me so Sonny can spend some more money with him in his joint. Me and the band finally agreed on a song I want to do. I was still young, so I had a lot of energy in me to do something electrifying. The only song I knew that everyone should've known how to play was James Brown's song *There Was a Time*. I knew I could stretch out to that song.

He began to introduce me saying, "Ladies and Gentlemen, you know Mr. Reuben has a tendency to find the best new talent in Las Vegas first. Here's a guy from St. Louis, Missouri. His name is Gene Anderson. How about a round of applause? He says he gonna rock the house. We gonna see what he has offer, okay?"

Everybody froze and paid attention because they thought I was a pimp. They had no idea I was an entertainer, thinking he better be good or we got some game for his ass. I knew that's what they were thinking, you could feel it in the air. I already came in the joint and upstaged everybody, causing so much commotion. These hoes talking about me stretching the story, making it longer than it truly was. Now I got to stand up for real, so I went up to the band, turned my back to the audience and said, "Let's do that song by James Brown, *There Was a Time*."

They said, "how do you want it?"

I said, "Man, kick it up another notch, put some heat up under it."

They said, "Come on wit it baby boy."

They counted out and the band was hitting it hard. The tempo was up there. I got to moving and did the James Brown moves, kicking, I put a whole show on. By that time the whole front row was rocking with me. Everyone was into it. I finally hit the words 'there was a time when I used to dance'. Boy when I hit that note I was right on queue, right on pitch, right on everything because I knew this was a very important moment for me.

I was out on front street and got this gig for myself. Sonny didn't give it to me, faith gave it to me, I think. I do believe that faith has a lot of importance in your life as well as influence in your life. So, I done rocked the house as best as I could. I was tired by then. I had interacted with the audience and had the people whooping and hollering and screaming. I felt good. I was back in my element. I didn't want that stigma of pimp associated with me, I wanted star associated with me. That's really where my heart is at.

So, when I got off the stage Mr. Reuben came to me and said, "Boy, you got something special. Why don't you come gig for me?"

I said, "Listen, I gotta go back and talk it over with Sonny first." Sonny is probably upset with me because I had been gone with his car this long. He might be worried because he don't know where I'm at or what I'm doing. I'm out here on my own so I gotta get back. I said, "Hey, let me get back to Sonny and have him come over here with me. Y'all talk it over about me working down here with you at your club."

He said, "That's cool man, you gone hang around here a while?"

I said, "Nah, I gotta get back over to the Stardust where Sonny is because he's probably worried about me, I've been gone a while."

He said, "Well, I'll get the bouncer to walk you out to the car man."

I thought it was a little strange but then it flashed in my head that the other girl and her boyfriend was going at it at the bar. He was upset because she didn't have the money she should've had for staying out with Sonny. He was probably trying to set me up to try to check me when I came outside. He knew he couldn't do shit to me in Mr. Reuben's place, and Mr.

Reuben knew this. He had seen it, because he sees everything. He knew that if something were to happen to me over there Sonny would've come over there and tore that place apart. He had probably done it before, like if he got mad that Reuben wouldn't give him any more credit or whatever, because Sonny was uncontrollable when he was on one of them binges.

So, he called the dude over, great big ole guy about 6'5 almost 300 pounds and a big ole pistol on his side. He took me out to the car there. The dude was with some henchman and the hoes, he was all huffing and puffing. When he seen me with the bouncer, he knew Reuben had already spotted what they were up to, and Reuben was gonna be responsible for me getting out of there. He had to get past this big ole bodyguard to get to me. Plus, this was the joint that all the pimps hung out at. He didn't want to get 86'd out the joint, so I guess he thought he would take it up another time.

I wasn't paying him no fucking attention, as young and brash as I was. I would've kicked the shit out him because I was hopped up and hype to the max, especially since I done broke these hoes. I went into the club, met the big man on the West Side, Mr. Reuben, sung and rocked the joint. I wasn't thinking about him. I got in the car and peeled rubber on his ass, cape flying in the air.

Soon as I arrived at the Stardust Hotel, would you believe Sonny was standing there in the doorway looking for the car, looking for me? I believed he didn't know if I had run off with his car or not because he didn't really know me. But he trusted me with the car. When I pulled up, he let out a sigh of total relief because he probably thought that something might have happened to me.

Whatever it was, he got into the car, "Geney baby, I was worried about you, you took so damn long." Then I began to tell him about the thing over there with Mr. Reuben, that I took the girls and dropped them off at Reuben's and I done the singing and all that, before I got back around to talking about the confrontation with the hoes. He looked at me with amazement like, damn boy, you sure enough got some heart. He was so proud of the fact I was able to go over there and go in a joint like Reuben's. I was able to get in there and rock the joint without confrontations. He knows that was a real bucket of blood joint, and that's where them hoes hang out that he already had the problem with at the hotel room. He felt like it was okay because he paid them off.

He was a little bit more sober by then, so we jumped in the ride and went to get something to eat, down there by Saharah Hotel. It was a baby back rib joint; he loved them baby back ribs. He said, "Hey man, I'm so glad you're here."

We pulled up in the parking lot and I say, "I got something to tell you man." I was a little reluctant to bring it up to him, I knew that eventually he's gonna find out about the truth of what went down. "You know you had me drop those hoes off."

He said, "Yeah Geney boy, you didn't have no problem getting over there did you?"

I said, "No. Listen, I didn't like the way they treated you Sonny boy. Before we got over there, they was talking shit in the car about you, like I wasn't even there. So, I pulled the car over, I stuck them hoes up, and I took back your money."

He said "You did what? You took-"

I said, "Yeah Sonny boy, I took your money man. I didn't take it all back, but I took back most of your money. And here it is." I gave him three hundred dollars of the money that I took from them hoes. He put his hand out and he looked at the money then looked at me. He had the strangest look on his face. I had never seen it on anybody's face before, like total disbelief. He was quiet for a moment like he was stunned. I didn't know what to think. Maybe I would get in trouble. This is the champ, so it might hit the paper that the champ sent somebody to hold up hoes, I don't know what to think.

All of a sudden, he looked me in the face and bust out laughing with that infectious laugh, "Geney boy, you something else, boy. Geney boy, you okay, boy. You my motherfuckin' man boy! Geney boy, I love you man." He just "Geney boy" me to death and kept laughing his ass off. He put me in a head lock; I'm fighting him off. He said, "Man, you keep the money."

He stuffed the money back in my pocket. He said, "You keep the money. You my motherfuckin' man." From that moment on, I felt in my heart Sonny knew he had a real friend in me.

Geney Boy

After that incident, and a little time had passed, I could tell I had gained Sonny's trust, his confidence more and more as a true friend. He would give me his money, all his money, man. I had $4000, $5,000 in my pocket. He gave me his rings. His rings was so big I couldn't even wear them on my thumb. I used to put them around my neck and on my chain. He gave me his rings, his money, even sometimes his pistol to hold on to.

He knew that the police would pull him over some time just for GP because it was him. But he was a little better off in Vegas than he was in Philadelphia and St. Louis and those other places he had stayed. Day after day it was the same thing over and over again. We ride the strip, I drive 3 to 5 miles an hour. Guys behind us in their cars blowing their horns. He stick his finger out the car drunk, "Fuck you Pussy!" I laugh because I wasn't no better. I was with Sonny. I was young and stupid. If that's what Sonny wanted to do I was cool. He said don't drive so fast. We weren't doing but 5 miles an hour, but he was talking like we would do 50 down the strip. I laughed my ass off. He laughed because he knew it was because he was drunk.

After a week, or a little bit more than a week passed we did the same thing over and over. I got tired of it plus, there was no talk about Sammy. I never got a chance to meet Sammy, and it seemed like all we were doing was getting high and partying, getting high and partying and fucking hoes. It was okay, but I was still married. I had a problem trying to explain every day to my wife what was going on. My mom was trying to really tell me that I had a young wife now. She was a beautiful girl. She was back home all alone with a very young baby and I'm out here with Sonny Liston. What am I doing to show her that I'm making some progress out here? I couldn't really tell them and just pleaded and begged. I would love to talk on the phone, and hope that she can understand.

I was sort of like Sonny. I was alone too, even though I was constantly surrounded by different people, but everybody wanted something from me, on my level. Everybody wanted something from Sonny on his level. It was all about what I could do for them just like what Sonny could do for those that was around him. And so, we had that kind of bond. I knew after I had spent time with Sonny that he needed me. If not me, he needed a guy that cared about him as I did that was qualified to protect him. He felt more comfortable around gang people when I was with him than he had ever before because he knew I was very alert. I was sharp and my concern was to look out for him. His whole concern was how he felt at that minute. He was going to have a good time. He didn't give a shit because he was going downhill.

I was always bragging about Sonny. He said, "Geney-boy, this ain't nothing. You should have been with me man when I was champ. When I was a champion, the whole world was right there man. You should have been with me Geney boy when I was champion." He would say that over and over and over and over. I believe in my heart that he really meant that because he was forever trying to show me things that he could do that I would be impressed by. It was like I had in that little bitty short time, grown as close to him as a baby brother or son or loving nephew or something. He always wanted to show me something. He wanted to impress me.

That was unusual because Sonny didn't give a shit about impressing nobody but Sonny Boy. He felt that the whole world had a wrong opinion of him, and he wasn't trying to prove nothing to the whole world. He was just trying to live his life the way he wanted to do it. He was strong enough as a tough guy and was hooked up with the mob and he didn't care. He just wanted to do whatever he wanted to do. The times when he wasn't training for a fight, or he wasn't really getting into some real higher echelon business or negotiations or something that was associated with his status, he just wants to just fuck hoes and party and stay drunk. That was because of frustration. I found out as time went on, Sonny wasn't really always like that, but he just couldn't drink. He takes two or three swallows, and he will be tore up.

I observed him more and more and he allowed himself to be more open to me. I began to see where people have taken advantage of him throughout his whole life. I'm very sharp and perceptive about what's going on around me and what made people tick, especially those that I was ultimately concerned with. At that point in time, my whole life was beginning to unfold and develop with my association with Sonny Liston. He had taken me to a level in which I couldn't even imagine, much less know what I was hoping I could get into. I wasn't familiar with something of that status. This was not the President of the United States, as he used to say, this is the former heavyweight champ of the world. It's a big world out here and he had been the number one man treated like that. He had been exposed, and he was allowing me to step into that world, not as a seeing eye dog for him, but as a close friend. To really see the truth about how it was and how he was being treated as a celebrity.

I had my day in the spotlight. I thought I had been a star, a little R&B Chitlin Circuit star. I was not up there on the level of the Sammy Davis's and the Sonny Liston's and the Muhammad Ali's and the Jim Brown's and the Robert Stack's and the Count Basie's. I've read about these guys and seen these guys on TV and dreamed about being one of these guys, but I was tossed out in the middle of all this with Sonny because of his status. The former heavyweight champion of the world was such a major, controversial figure that he used to keep my mind on a constant roller coaster.

I was constantly trying to adjust to that situation, worried about my family at home because I loved my family. That was the purpose of me going into this deep water. I made such a major move in my life to be able to supply my loved ones with the things I thought that I was capable of providing for them, being out here in Las Vegas with a person of Sonny Liston status. But now it seemed that all I was doing was riding up and down the strip or going into these little dinky clubs, finding no good, slut-ass hoes, and freaking out with them with Sonny.

Now I'm beginning to show frustration. I didn't come out here to do what we be doing day after day after day. Sonny began to get the message by my body language about things that I wasn't as impressed by as I had been when I very first got there. He began to see the difference in my approach to things and my lack of enthusiasm for a lot of the straight bullshit that I really wasn't interested in. I wanted to see him do bigger things. I knew that he was qualified for more than just riding down the strip and hanging out, people laughing at him, fucking with him. He was joking with folks it was fun and good times. All the prize fighters I know up to this day has this wild, rambunctious streak inside of them that they just have to let loose when they're not in training. Sonny was absolutely that way, so after a while we wound up in front of the Stardust. We drove up and down the strip from one end to the other and it had gotten late, and not a hoe was in sight. The doorman opened up the door and Sonny slowly struggled to get out the car.

He was blasted this time. I rushed around to help get him out the door. People were looking at him, knowing who he was. I was telling him, "Put your stomach in, man, put your stomach in." So, he pulled his stomach in and smiled at the people, and they wanted his autograph, whether drunk or not. So, they gave him a little piece of paper, and he grabbed it with his big old hands. He could barely hold the pencil in his big old hands. He wrote *Sonnyboy Liston*, then he pulled the doorman over to the side and whispered something in his ear.

Apparently, it was to the effect of finding him a new girl tonight. And what I meant by new girl is that Sonny had a phonebook, a little black book full of numbers of girls that he dated before. But if it was in his power, he never wanted the same girl twice. He always wanted a new girl. He said "Gene baby, it ain't nothing but two kinds of hoes. A great big old good one, and a good old big one." He burst out laughing.

I laugh my ass off because Sonny was actually funnier than fuck. But in my heart, I kind of felt sorry for him because a lot of what he was doing at that particular time was really trying to impress me. He thought that would make me happy because I was a country boy out of St. Louis who had never seen nothing before. And this was sort of like the big hurrah for me coming from him.

And that ain't what I really was about, I really didn't care about anything because I've been a little star all my life. I had girls here and there and everywhere but, once again, I was trying to be faithful to my wife. I was hoping that would make her be faithful to me by being so far away. So, I really felt sad about that whole issue. But nevertheless, he still was trying to book some dates for both of us. He had me to pay a Bellman $100 to send a girl up from the hotels dating service because the hotel had whores. We walked through the lobby and people looked at him. The dealers and the pit bosses and staff looking at him laughing under their breath. 'There he goes.' No telling what he's going to do tonight because Sonny was known to tear casinos up when he got drunk.

So, we staggered and struggled our way to the elevator. I guess they had a sigh of relief when they saw us get on the elevator, heading up to the penthouse. We got the key for the elevator and got up to the penthouse. I opened the door and there was Bobby Tunstall, from St. Louis, with his whole set of pearl drums in the middle of the floor. I couldn't believe my eyes.

I was so happy to see somebody that I knew. Because I had been doing so many different things that was so foreign to me. And I had nobody that was really my age, or nobody to discuss doing some of things with. Sonny was so much older than me and felt like Mr. Sonny Liston. And seeing Bobby was just a joy. But the first thing that crossed my mind was how in the hell did he get to Las Vegas? Sonny saw him and said, "Who in the fuck is this?"

"Sonny boy, this is my friend Bobby Tunstall, one of the guys in my band in St. Louis." He calmed down a little bit, but he surprised Sonny especially with all his drums in the floor and everything. Sonny thought they done gave the suite to somebody else and we got locked out. They had the key and got in. And he was gonna go downstairs and tear the joint up because he knew that suite belonged to him. Yale Korn gave that suite to him. Somebody down at that desk fooled around and made a bad mistake. And he was drunk enough to cause a major problem. But after he cooled down, he realized that this young guy was really my friend. They had let him in the room because he told them that Sonny was our manager. And I was with him. And they have seen me with Sonny so often. They knew that it was another young guy hanging out with Sonny, so they believed what Bobby said.

So, Bobby Tunstall was a spoiled young kid that came from an aristocratic family. He was the only son, and they treated him like royalty. To be truthful, he was a little spoiled brat. Bobby was a good guy, a very decent person. He was a little bit harder than you may have given him credit for. But he really did have nerve because it took a lot for me to jump out and come to Las Vegas. Nobody knew he was coming, and he didn't know anybody but hoped that he was gonna find me and he did. Bob's mother was one of those ladies that stuck behind her son, and she knew that he had stardom in him. She pushed him and pushed him and whatever it took for him to be able to get to the point of stardom she was willing to do. She worked at a local TV station down in St. Louis, channel five, and had a lot of influence. So, she kept us on TV when we was youngsters coming up and the band we was in.

It was four of us. Richard Martin was the guitar player. Paul Jackson was the bass player. Bobby Tunstall was the drummer, and me. There were all sorts of guys that played around with us like David Ham on trumpet, and Charles Hayes sometime on saxophone. But basically, it was the four of us, Richard Martin, Paul Jackson, me, and Bobby Tunstall. Richard and Paul were more or less comrades because they both played guitars and bass. Bobby was a good drummer, but he hadn't developed himself at that time. He turned out to be damn near Max Roach. He turned out to be a magnificent drummer in the end, but during those days he was just coming along. Richard and them wanted to be big time. They abandoned us and went off with a guy named Marcus Kelly, I think. I'm not sure but they went to some army base in Salt Lake City, Utah, or somewhere in Utah. They had a regular gig that left us.

It didn't really matter to me because I knew my mind was made up to come with Sonny. Bobby didn't know what he was going to do and his mother always felt that the opportunity was going to come for everybody but Bobby. She knew that I was like the tape that was holding his body together. She knew that I would take care of her Bobby if he got to where I was. So, she bought him a ticket, called around to all the hotels, and found out where we were, put him on a plane in sent him.

Somewhere in the situation, I calmed Sonny down and told him the whole story about how Richard and them had abandoned us. Bobby was a good guy. He was so close. I talked him into letting Bobby stay. So, first thing Sonny did after he straightened up a little bit he looked at the drums and looked at Bobby and say, "Aye boy, can you play them drums?"

Bobby standing there looking like he's got to pee in his clothes. He said, "Yes."

I told Sonny he can really play. He said, "Let me hear you play."

Bobby got up on those drums and that's when the Max Roach came out of him for the very first time. I got to give him credit. He played his ass off. As long as we had been there as a band out in the streets, he had never played that good before. He did Precious Rose flam paradiddle [drum pattern]. I mean, he must have been at home practicing his ass off after we left knowing that his mom was going to send him out there where we were. And boy he had improved 50% if not more, from the time I just left St. Louis until the time he showed up there in Las Vegas.

Sonny was so impressed he said, "Move over, let me see him." He got on the drums laughing like a sum bitch.

The security guard came to the door and said, "Mr. Liston, y'all are making too much noise. The other guests are complaining."

Sonny grabbed him in the collar and said, "Get the fuck up out of here. Don't you see the band in here practicing?" He slammed the door in his face and went back and started beating on drums more. I fell out on the floor laughing. Bobby was just standing there like a little kid who didn't know what to do. He was still looking at Sonny like wow, this is Sonny Liston. And this is a big old motherfucker too, he's about to cry.

He was scared Sonny was going to bust his drums because Sonny was beating the shit out of them. This must have been great therapy for Sonny because when he got to beat the drums and laughed with us, he relaxed a little bit. It seemed for the first time in years he really didn't feel intimidated, and he didn't have to intimidate anyone. It was a legitimate Big Uncle Friendship, and I could see it in his face. I believe he was relaxed and genuinely happy. He was laughing and having a really good time.

We laughed and joked around for a little while and the phone rang. It was the doorman from downstairs telling Sonny that the girl was there from the dating service and was it okay to send her up? I let her in, and she looked haggard. I thought to myself, this bitch ain't worth no 100 dollars. Sonny looked at her, walked right past her, opened the door, and looked out. He said, "Where the girl at?"

She said, "I'm the girl."

He said, "No, you ain't bitch. Where yo' old ass come from?"

She got insulted and said, "Well, Mister Liston, they told me to come up and you will be my date tonight. You and your friends."

He said, "Well this all they got, fuck that."

He put her ass out. I couldn't believe it. He was just as cold and blatant about it. She went back downstairs and the doorman calls. He says, "Mr. Liston, the young lady said that you didn't give her money, and you didn't treat her right."

Sonny said, "Listen man, why would you send me some old tore up haggard old White woman? I know you got some better girls down there. You sent me better girls before."

He said, "Well, a lot of the girls are scared to come up especially when you treat them like you doing. Not only that, but it's also late, Mr. Liston. This is all we got available for you tonight."

Sonny said, "Well, if that's the case keep that bitch for yourself," and slammed the phone down. Me and Bobby were rolling on the floor laughing because he was just showing off for us. He busts out laughing himself and the three of us were making so much noise that the windowpane was vibrating. He pulled out a joint and we started smoking some more weed.

Then Sonny came up with the bright idea to go to Roover's to party and fuck some whores over there.

Trip to Rueben's

We finally made it over to Rueben's. It was raining that night and the guy that was normally the bouncer was out parking cars. He saw us and met Sonny with an umbrella. Everyone was so excited when they saw Sonny get out of the car.

He was drunk as a skunk, stumbling over things and cracking jokes. He was straight showing out for me and Bobby, and we were showing out for him too. He could tell I was happy because I had my homeboy with me. He knew that I needed someone with me that was more my age to hang with. Bobby was the perfect person because Sonny liked him. Bobby was a young guy that had good manners, and Sonny liked good, polite people around him. He really had a lot of discipline about him and had good manners. He was someone that liked to represent our race and represent his profession in a certain manner, even though he would act like a straight heathen himself. He always wanted to see the gentleman come out in us, but he likes us as players too now.

We were constantly trying to give him what he wanted in order for us to be able to continue on the journey we thought we were going to embark upon. Now not only did he have me, but he also had Bobby. He had two sidekicks that he was happy with and was comfortable around. So, the party was really on. We walked through the door, and it was like electricity in the place. Sonny Liston was in the building. The band started playing as they did everywhere we went. Boy, he got to dancing in the aisle and talking loud, people were paying attention to him. They were getting his autograph, and he really felt comfortable because he was in his element. He was right in his zone.

Bob Bailey spotted us and rushed right over to Sonny. He looked just like a fashion statement. He had on a milk white linen suit with brown and white spectator shoes on. He was really tall and sophisticated looking, had wavy hair and everybody just adored him at that time. In the 60s, that was a great, great look. So, Bob and Sonny grabbed each other and hugged each other like two lost fraternity brothers. Bob says to Sonny, "Hey I see you back over here slumming man, we ain't seen you in a long time."

Sonny replied, "Yeah man, I been out on the wagon. I had some real big things to do but now I'm out loose and partying and I got my boys with me."

Bob looks over and says, "Yeah that's the young fella that came over here and turned this joint out. Yeah, that's Geney boy."

Sonny says, "And this is his friend Bobby. Give us a good seat, man, and send me some girls over." Bob was always a diplomat. He gave the celebrities everything they needed to keep coming and keep his place one of the premier spots on the West Side, and to keep the right stars around him.

Bob placed us over in the VIP section and I saw my man, Lou Rawls. He was there with two White girls, looking like a king. He saw Sonny. He was one of Sonny's biggest fans. "Sonny boy, Sonny boy," he hollered. They hugged each other and got to talking loudly. Lou introduced him to the girls he was with, and Sonny introduced me to Lou. I was just like flabbergasted cause Lou Rawls has always been one of my favorite stars and ironically after all the years went by, he and I became extremely good friends.

We finally sat down and started grooving with the band and here comes Mr. Bailey with three fine girls. One of them I was just looking at her and straight drooling. She had on a long red wig, and she wore all red with a mid-short tight mini skirt. Man, I was young and horny for her like you would never believe. Bobby was just sitting there with his mouth wide open cause he just didn't know what to do. Sonny was laughing at both of us because we was like two country boys loose like a bull in a china closet. We was capping at him and talking loud and talking fast. Sonny was spending more time laughing at what we were doing than he was with the girl. She was all over him, hands all around his back playing with his dick up under the table and the whole nine yards.

Somewhere within the madness, he waved at Bob to come over to the table and told him, "Hey, let my boys do a tune with the band." Bob jumped on top of that cause he knew I had already rocked that joint one time, and it was packed that night. He went over to the bandstand, and he whispered something in the band leader's ear. He came back and told Sonny that the band leader would be over in a minute and talk to me about what I wanted to do.

Man, I was so excited because I was gonna get a chance to sing in front of Sonny again over here at the real players joint for the stars there. Lou Rawls and Count Basie was hanging out at the time. All the big stars was hanging out over there. I was getting a chance to sing with Sonny sitting at the table with us and all the girls. I had my boy Bobby, my drummer, to come play with me. He knew all the breaks for me when I make a move, dip, spin or whatever. He knew how to keep up with me with the drums. I knew tonight we was gonna rock this joint if we were ever gonna do it in life.

I looked over at Sonny, and he appeared to be more nervous than me. He kept asking me over and over again, "Is you ready? What you gonna do, is you ready?"

I said, "Yeah Sonny, I got it, don't worry about it man, we fitting to rock this joint."

Boy he had a look on his face like he was so proud of me because I wasn't scared. Man, and I know, no doubt about it, I was his boy by then. He knew that Bobby had my back up on that stage. So, he began to really start laughing with that infectious laugh.

People was looking at us and them hoes was just giggling and carrying on. Sonny was pouring vodka, and we was talking loud and the party was going on. It was just a great fun night man. All of a sudden, the guy called me up to the bandstand. It seemed like the walk from the bandstand was 100 miles away. All kinds of stars were all over the place. I started recognizing them and it was like man, this is gonna be a thrill to pull this one off. In my heart I knew I had every bit of confidence in the world to do what I was there to do, to rock this joint.

Sonny looked at me like, "Go get'em baby, go get'em."

The guy in the bandstand gave us a big announcement as if we was coming from the moon. I whispered in his ear what I wanted to do. Bobby got up on the drums and I walked up to the mic. I made an announcement where we were from, and that we was with Sonny and I said, "Sonny get up. Ladies and Gentlemen, Sonny Liston, The Heavy Weight Champion of the world". He waved his hand. People just applauded and hollered for him. Then I acknowledged Lou Rawls and the people started applauding him. Man, I felt like I was on TV. I did the song by the Temptations, *Ain't too proud to beg*. They hit the song too. *"I know you want to leave me, but I refuse to let you go."* And when I hit that note like that, the girls got to hollering.

Man, we rocked that joint. Sonny and the girls was dancing at the table, and the people was up on the floor. I felt good, man. I could see that Sonny was having the time of his life. Man, we didn't let him down. You could tell it was the night of all nights and for him and for us.

We did a couple more songs and we finally came down off the bandstand and Sonny almost ran over everybody to hug us up. The people was just patting us on the back like they had seen what they had come there for. The party was on. Man, Bob came over to our table and it was straight excitement. Man, Lou Rawls came over and said, "Sonny man, the boys was hot man, and so if you get a chance, come on down over to my show. Bring them with you." I was like, Lou Rawls invited us to his show! Man, it was like we was in entertainment heaven, I guess.

So, Sonny told Bob he was gonna manage us and do some big things and he wanted to put us on his TV show. Bob gave us a date to come to the TV show. We partied some more, gathered up the girls, and went up on the strip to the hotel. The freaking began again, over and over again all night. The next day we partied. Bobby was about to get worried because it was a whole new experience for him. As far as I was concerned, I was through with it too because we had gotten off track. All I was thinking about was making Sonny happy. Sonny wanted to party, Sonny wanted to freak, but then Sonny realized he had more to do too. He was running out of money and not only that, but he also hadn't been home in 2 or 3 weeks.

We had been partying ever since he picked me up from the airport. We moved out of the penthouse of the Stardust into some bungalows that was $100 a week. The penthouse was costing him up the ying-yang even though we initially got comfortable in there. So, a little time passed, and Sonny began to sober up. You could tell the difference when he was under the influence of that Smirnoff vodka and when he was just the Sonny Liston everybody knew as a responsible person. He began to get quieter and quieter. Sonny was an introvert when he was sober because he was a very deep thinker. He thought about things four or five times before he said it or did it and he was very precise about whatever he was planning to do. So, he grabbed me up one day and he said, "Hey Geney boy, I'm going home, and I want to take you home with me man. Maybe Geraldine won't be so upset with me being out so long when she see you."

And that was the first time he had mentioned her since I met him. I didn't know anything about her, but I knew he was married. So, we jumped in the Cadillac and rode over to the residential section of Las Vegas. A nice little section where there was nothing but ranch-style houses where stars and millionaires, pit bosses and gangsters lived. It was on the Stardust golf course. I think the name of the street was Ottawa Drive. When we pulled up, it was a white house, and you had to walk down the sidewalk from the garage. There was a long, winding sidewalk that led you to a little porch. You could enter the house upstairs in the basement. We went in through the den and when he shut the door, I heard someone say, "Charles is that you?" And that was the first time I had ever seen Geraldine Liston.

Boy she lit into him and was crying and screaming and hollering at him. I'm saying to myself, "Man what have I walked into?" Sonny had stayed out with me longer than he had ever stayed away from home or from her, partying with me. I thought he did this all the time, but how wrong I was. From that day on, she never really liked me. She thought I had the influence on Sonny to make him do what she probably knew that he was always doing when he was drunk. He was never out that long, so she thought that I was influencing him to do these things.

To be truthful, nobody, I mean absolutely nobody, could influence Sonny to do nothing that he really didn't want to do in his heart. She still felt I may have been a bad influence on Sonny like most of the people he was dealing with, typically from the west side of town. These are the Black people that he was so partial to. He was always trying to impress and to help these people. So, Sonny walked up the steps beside me on a little sneaky tip. Man, you could hear her crying, "Oh Sonny boy, what you been doing? *Woo woo woo.*"

The first time I heard a little voice say, "PaPa, PaPa." And that was the first time I met his adopted son, Daniel.

Daniel was a beautiful little kid. I think he must have been about eight or ten years old, but I don't know for sure. He came down the steps and saw me, and he liked me right away. We shook hands and got to talking. Sonny had impregnated a girl over in Sweden or Switzerland or somewhere in the Netherlands. She had a son and sent him to America on his own to be with Sonny. So, Sonny and Geraldine adopted him, and he was Sonny's world. Sonny loved the kid, and the kid loved Sonny. He had a little accent, and it used to make Sonny laugh so much because he would say things so uniquely.

So, he showed me around the den. I was like a kid in a candy store. I had never seen such wonderful new and unique things. Sonny was a major collector. He collected things from everywhere he had been around the world, and I was a ghetto kid. I had never seen all these new foreign things. I had seen movies, books, and some people who had a lot of stuff, but this time I was in the mix of it all and I was so impressed. I looked around the walls and there were pictures of Sonny with all kinds of big names like President Kennedy and Jim Brown. He had them over the entire wall like a boarder.

In the middle of the floor there was a big, huge stuffed bear. He said some people gave that to him when he was getting ready to fight Muhamad Ali because they used to call him the bear. He loved that bear image. He would act like he didn't particularly care for it, but that image of being a great big strong bear was cool with him. That is when I started calling him Baha. He loved it when I called him Baha because I made him sound tough. Anything tough was okay with Sonny because he was extremely macho.

So, Daniel took me by the hand, and out by the pool. Man, it was a big, huge Olympic size pool right on the golf course. He had side fences, but he didn't have an end fence because as you sit down in the lounge chairs, you could see the entire golf course. It was beautifully manicured and everything. I thought, man I didn't even have any grass in my neighborhood let alone a yard that swept up into a golf course. Daniel and I slept in the chairs. We rushed upstairs and got cookies and stuff.

I began to be his big boy. He was so lonely because he only had Sonny and Geraldine. Only a few privileged kids in the neighborhood could play with him occasionally. He was really just a young kid who was thirsty for friendship, and I was this big boy. In time I became a big brother to him, and he loved me, and I loved him. He was such a great little kid, but he was a little spoiled brat as well. Sonny had spoiled him to the tenth power. There was no other person that Sonny trusted or loved but his wife and his kid.

Everyone that Sonny knew was just playing on who he was throughout his entire life. As you know, Sonny had a very difficult life growing up and now he was being surrounded by new people that he really felt comfortable around which absolutely included me. And for him to bring me home knowing how Sonny was as a person was more than a privilege. It was something that appeared as total trust and love for a person. In time I realized this because I saw how Sonny was so standoffish with most people. Sonny probably had some very bad experiences with people, so he didn't take up with too many people at all. Matter of fact, it's like the old cliché says, "If you pick up a frozen snake and you put him in your bosoms and you thaw him out, sooner or later he's gonna bite you. You should have known he was gonna do this because he was a snake." So, Sonny was with that philosophy. He never took too many people to his bosom in life.

I must have been an exception because there I was sitting in Sonny Liston's house. I came all the way from St. Louis, talked to him all those months on the phone, and I was finally there. He introduced me to all the people I met. He really took to me as though I was a son of his, as though I was a friend of his. I loved the fact that his trust in me was unique and different than all of those I had seen around him, and even those I hadn't known that he was familiar with. I tried to keep myself from that perspective.

I loved Daniel as I began a great step towards gaining his confidence. This was his decision, allowing me to be sincere and being around his family. Daniel started pulling out his toys man, and we was playing with his toys. He had all kinds of expensive, unique toys that I had never seen. We were having a ball down there. Sonny came down and saw that Daniel and I had bonded right away. That made him so happy man. Daniel just grabbed him and kissed him and rode his knee and stuff saying, "Papa."

I felt so good to know that Sonny had a very warm and loving family around him, but Geraldine was just like the witch from hell as far as I was concerned. She rolled her eyes at me and looked at me as if she could see straight through me. She was really looking at the wrong thing because I was nothing like what she thought. She was judging me for being like the people that she had encountered from the West Side. Sonny had somehow let their paths cross, and she didn't like me at all. But I was still Sonny's friend, and she was always a congenial hostess.

Geraldine fixed some sandwiches and stuff. We sat out by the pool and Daniel and I played with his toys. Sonny and I took a look around the golf course. He showed me who lives here and who lives there. I asked him about the golf balls and did the golf balls ever come over the house. He said, "Yeah, they in the pool. The pool is full of golf balls." We laughed. It was just a wonderful occasion. Then we partied a little bit more and we talked.

It was time for me to go the hotel so Sonny told Geraldine that he was gonna drop me off and he would be right back. She wasn't going for that because she knew Sonny. She knew that if he got out of the house it was gonna be the same thing that it was before he had come home after being gone for so long. She started arguing with him. Then they went upstairs.

I was saying my last goodbyes to Daniel. We started walking towards the door from down in the den. I was talking and I was tickling him, and we were having a great time.

All of a sudden, I heard somebody say, "Run Geney boy, run!" I looked outside and Sonny said, "She gonna shoot us — run Geney boy run!" I looked up and she was standing in the doorway crying saying, "Sonny you son of a bitch," with a gun in her hand. I break out running, he breaks out running and she shoots, *POW, POW*. We are running our ass off.

I'm saying, "Man, what's going on?"

Sonny says, "Man I don't know what's happening. All of a sudden, she is yelling, 'Sonny boy, you son of a bitch!', crying and carrying on and shooting." She goes back to the house. I finally catch up with him and he starts laughing his ass off saying, "Man, you know that crazy ass woman is fixin' to shoot us so let's get the hell out of here."

So, we tipped back to the car and drove off as fast as we could. He's laughing his ass off because he knew in his heart she could have shot us if she wanted to. She was just blowing off steam. That's just the way she was. We drove back over to the West Side, and he started introducing me to some guys over there that he knew.

Everybody was just so glad to see Sonny. Sonny was a very well-loved person in the neighborhood. There were times when Sonny fed families that didn't have food. He was like Robin Hood. Everybody knew over there when they saw Sonny, they could get something from him. Sonny paid their insurance, their rent, fed them, bought shoes for the kids to go to school, all that. They would find out where he was at, and damn near line up for something from Sonny and he would give it to them, especially if he was drunk. They could take his shoes off him and it didn't make him no difference because he was a very generous person.

With some people, he would straight kick them in their ass if they walked up to him because he did have a hard passion against pimps. He didn't like pimps and people in that world on a small level.

So, we went into the casino I think was the Tom Tavern. That was the first time I had seen the game Keno. Sonny said Keno was sort of like Bingo, but the Chinese bought the game over to America if I remember correctly. They would mark the board with a felt pen really fast, and it was very exciting. If you hit the numbers, you could make a lot of money with the Keno. Sonny introduced me to the Chinamen that was running Keno and all the pit bosses.

Man, I was feeling really good. I was Sonny's boy. He finally had a friend that he could hang out with and show things to. It was always something new that he could present to me that I would feel good about it and I got enthusiastic about it. It would motivate him more and more and more. I just knew that he needed a friend. People would ask him who I was, and he would tell them jokingly that "This is my bodyguard."

They would look at me and say, "This little son of a bitch ain't no bodyguard."

He would tell them, "Yeah he's a Karate expert — try him, try him." By him being Sonny Liston, they sort of believed him. And Sonny knew that I was pretty tough anyway, so he didn't hesitate to say that. The word on the streets got out that Sonny's got a bodyguard. A little half pint bodyguard at that and he's a Taekwondo, Judo, and black belt Karate expert. Man, what did he do that for? From then on, everybody thought that I was a real triple threat and a terror. The word had gotten out from those hoes that we had when we first got there that I was a dangerous person to be dealing with that was with Sonny. They tied all that together and really believed it. Sonny wanted them to believe it so they would not approach me in any kind of way that was dangerous to me if he didn't happen to be around. So, I played the role.

After he showed me around a little bit more and introduced me to a few more little people, we got back in the car headed back to the Stardust apartments. Bobby was there by himself and knowing him as I did, I was almost sure he was about to panic. In the meantime, we was scraping for cash. Sonny had spent money like a wild man. I found out later on, he got a $10,000 a month allowance from his accountant for his own personal expenses. Sonny had gone through that $10,000 allowance as fast as a race car at an Indiana speedway.

On the way back to the apartment he stopped by a friend's house. An old small time mob guy named Eddie Turner. He was a typical Italian looking guy, hair slicked back with a long-penciled mustache, and he was a real sleezy-looking guy. He was Sonny's boy, but Sonny told me that he was very slick so be careful with him. They did a little small-time dirty deal together and he owed Sonny some money. So, Sonny stopped by his house to see if he could collect his money. He introduced me to Eddie we began a little small talk about where I was from and what I was doing.

I asked him about the house. It was a nice little house, and I thought that maybe I could buy me a little house like that. It wasn't elaborate like Sonny's, but it was a nice little house. And he told me he homesteaded the house. I had never heard that word. In other words, the government couldn't take it cause he is utilizing it as an old homestead or something like that. I tried to understand it for the longest, but it finally came to me that he hadn't planned on paying for the house. So that confirmed that he was a slick guy just as Sonny had said.

He and Sonny went into the backroom and left me in the living room for a little bit. When Sonny came out, I realized Sonny was doing some things that he didn't want me to know. We got back in the car, and

I started to ask him questions about Eddie. He finally told me that Eddie had a little sack, and he was selling a little cocaine and a small spot of heroin. Eddie was selling primarily to get some cash.

During those days, blowing and tooting was the in thing. Guys had spoons around their necks. Gold spoons, double gold spoons, all kinds of paraphernalia like that, and a little bottle with the cocaine in it. It was that era. I personally had never had any of that and wasn't really interested in it.

Sonny had a little more money to work with and we was headed to the hotel to pick up Bobby. We made one more stop to another guy that owed Sonny some money. Sonny explained different ways he was getting money, and it was a game they called Shylocking. Shylocking was loaning a person money, and they had to pay you a percentage over the money that they borrowed. We went to this guy's house and when he saw Sonny, you seen fear in his face because it was apparent that he didn't have all of Sonny's money. Sonny was the kind of person that you couldn't play with about money. At this time, Sonny was kinda sober and he was kinda dangerous. The guy was explaining to Sonny why he didn't have his money and Sonny pointed to me. "See this guy right here, this is my new bodyguard. If you don't have my money, I'm a send him back and turn him loose on you and you really don't want that."

Now I'm saying to myself, "I'm the littlest guy in the room. Wonder why he say that?" But I had his pistol in my waist, and the guy could see the pistol. When he saw the pistol, he figured what Sonny said was true. Knowing who he was, and the kind of people Sonny was affiliated with, he had no clue that I really wasn't dangerous at all. He had a straight melt down about that. So he went into the bedroom, went through some clothes or something, and came up with at least a couple hundred dollars. Sonny said he wanted his money, and he cursed him and said, "I want my fucking money, and I want it now. I be back tomorrow and pick it up."

He said, "I get it for you Sonny boy, I get it for you Sonny boy."

We got back to the car; he bust out laughing. He says, "I scared that son of a bitch." We laughed and laughed about it. We headed back over to the hotel where Bobby was, to the back of Stardust hotel. There the brown bungalows were back there — one bedroom, two bedrooms, three bedrooms, like small apartments.

Band Reunion, then Down to Two

When we went to the door, Bobby was all excited and I couldn't understand why. I thought we was gonna be bent out of shape because we had left him for such a long time. I know he was sorta pampered and scared. He had talked to Richard and Paul, the other part of the band who had run off and gone to the Air Force base to play. He told him where we was, and they wanted to come so the whole band could get back together again.

Sonny didn't really understand what that meant at first. I explained to Sonny that I could be so much better if I had my original band, and could he help me bring them there. We did have the apartment so we could really put the band together. He would be great managing us. We could make some money, and he could book us on a lot of shows and stuff.

It seemed like I made some sense to him, and he really was trying to satisfy me, because he really did love me. I was like a son to him because no one had been fair with him. He thought a lot of me so if that was gonna make me happy and be a benefit to the way he wanted to present me, he said it's okay for them to come. Man, we was both excited about it, Bobby and I. Man, I called Richard back and we were screaming and laughing on the phone and carrying on. I could see it in my mind because I knew we had a great group. This town hadn't seen nothing like we was trying to do before we left St. Louis. I knew this was going to be something fresh and new in the area.

It was a small group, just four of us and Richard was an extremely talented musician. Richard could play that guitar. I believe to this day he was one of the best guitar players I have ever known. He could play rhythm as well as lead at the same time as if he was two people. It was no conflict in musical interest. He was a great, but his attitude was fucked up. He thought he was a good as he was, and he tried to appear to be better as a person, and he was really an asshole. As a musician, he would try to make that be an excuse for his attitude. But he was really one of the greatest.

Paul the base player, he was just the opposite as far as personality was concerned. Paul was an extreme perfectionist, and every note had to be in the right place. All the chords had to be perfect, and he was very regimented. Richard would play chords around Paul, which Paul wasn't familiar with. Richard had gone to college for guitar, so he was a little light eared. If you really want me to be truthful, Paul was the best bass player out of our area.

We put Sonny on the phone with Paul and Richard and let them talk to him. They were so excited to talk to the true Sonny Liston. So we asked what's it gonna take to get them down here. Richard as usual overplayed what it was gonna cost, so Sonny sent it to him, and they worked their way down to Las Vegas.

I conned Sonny into taking him a nap. We all lay down and went to sleep. The next day he was bright-eyed and bushy-tailed to see the agent about the gig. We go down there to Circus Circus. We got scheduled to do the gig about a week later. We did domestic stuff until we got ready for the gig, rehearsed over and over again in the apartment.

Sonny was the biggest critic. He said, "Man, we need to get a White boy in the band."

I said, "Sonny, we don't need no White boy in the band."

"Listen Geney boy, you don't know this town like I do. We need a White boy in the band to look good because they ain't gone buy an all-Black band in Las Vegas."

He was absolutely right, so he went and found us an Italian boy named Tony. He was good looking youngster. I liked him, and we got along really good. Richard and them didn't care too much for him because he was a phony. He couldn't play, he couldn't sing, so we wouldn't plug him in. Sonny even brought him a guitar. He couldn't play so we just muted the mike, muted the guitar, and we did all the hard singing. He would just sit there and lip sync and wiggle like Elvis Presley and play the guitar. It made us look good.

So, we finally got around to the day we did the gig, with the vanilla fudge. Man, we got up there and did all kinds of tricks and shit. I danced and split, danced and sang, we did the Jimmy Hendrix shit and stuff. We wore their asses out. We gigged over there for about a week with them in the Circus Circus, our first gig in Las Vegas.

After that, the agent got us an audition with a guy named Dave Dickerson, who was the entertainment director over at Caesars Palace. Through him and Sonny we got an audition in there. Man, we was excited like you wouldn't believe. Sonny was in seventh heaven because he thought it might be a chance for him to have a hard, explosive group that could be a great money thing for him.

At the time money was really big for groups. He had connections, and his fighting days looked like they was coming to an end. He wasn't getting the fights that he used to get. His managers and stuff was concentrating on George Foreman; they wasn't concentrating on him. He used to have a lot of static with them about that. People were offering him mediocre things, and he didn't appreciate that because he knew he still had a little something left in him. He also knew he had done a lot of favors, and he was deserving favors in return, but you know when the lights dim, the rats run away. Knowing that Sonny wasn't getting the attention that he was supposed to be getting from those on his level, he really concentrated hard on trying to make something for us.

But Richard seemed to have a whole other agenda. This girl he had got up with was around him all the time. She was really trying to get him off to herself so they could freak off or whatever, like all the time. Then Richard missed rehearsals, and Sonny was upset. In his heart Sonny knew this wasn't gonna work but he tried. I knew it wouldn't work because Richard had already shown his true colors. Paul and them was consistently arguing over that because Paul was really tired of Richard and his shit. So, the day finally came for us to do the audition at Caesars Palace. The agent came, the White boy came, we all set up our stuff and the stage was just huge. We should've had a full band or something because the stage was so huge we looked like ants on the stage.

The big boys was sitting in the audience, just like in the movies. Dave Dickerson, his boss, and some more mobsters because Sonny invited a whole lotta guys. I wasn't nervous, but I knew the group wasn't tight like we had been before because we didn't have unity. Then we had this White boy that didn't know the music at all, and he was just fronting for the look of it. Sonny could tell I was upset with that, he was steady trying to pump me up, telling me I can do it.

We finally got a chance, took our place on stage and we took off. Man, when we took off, we started playing our ass off. We was looking good and all of a sudden, I did a triple spin, and I fell. Boom, I hit the floor in the middle of the song. That was so fucking embarrassing. I got up and said that's okay and I tried it again and fell again. Twice, back-to-back. I knew it was over with from there. So, we just slipped on off the rest of the show.

We got off stage and the guy says, "You got a lot of energy, huh?"

I said, "Yeah I was just nervous today," but he didn't give us the shot. Sonny was trying to pep me up, but I was just trying so hard and carrying too much weight on my shoulders.

The guy, Mr. Dickerson, gave us the power of the pen that night. We ate at the Bacchanal, and a chance to go to the Patula Clark show, with George Kirby. So we went to the Bacchanal, and during those days you had to be dressed. They gave us all neckties, and you had to be absolutely dressed to go to those kinds of places. The violin players had milk white violins, a milk white piano was turning around in the middle of the floor. They was playing the same song and all of a sudden, they disbursed from off the stage. They walked off the platform through the audience, just like breathing, it was so elaborate. I never dreamed of seeing anything like that. All of us were country boys and were looking at it like what the fuck going on?

Sonny was laughing because he was trying to explain what was going on to us. They fed us a ten-course meal, but everything was dipped in some type of cognac or wine, even ice cream. We start eating ourselves high. Paul gets drunk on the food and the wine, and him and Richard get to arguing. They actually had a fight in the Bacchanal, five-star restaurant in Caesars Palace. Sonny was through with it from there. He grabbed them and shook 'em up, and the people was looking at us. Man, it was an ugly scene. Richard was telling Paul that he didn't need him and used him to get to Las Vegas to do what he wanted. Because everyone was upset about the audition, they got into a squabble. Right then I knew Sonny was through with that.

I was wondering like, I went through all this trouble to get these guys out here, we blew our first shot. We are fighting amongst ourselves, and all this ghetto shit is going on right in the middle of my greatest opportunity. I should've just did it by myself. So, we get back to the hotel, Sonny takes me to the side and says, "Geney baby, let me tell you something, these guys aint gonna work out for us. I'm gonna send them back home. I'm just gonna take you. Me and you just gonna roll up something, and I'm gonna make sure I get you where you want to go."

He knew my heart was just so broke, cause I was so upset with me falling, and he knew I was good enough to do it. I did that turn a thousand times, in those days, I was almost a ballerina, without even trying. But I was so uptight with so much squabbling always going on. The happy days just disappeared. I didn't want him to send them home, but I knew there wasn't no other shot. It was either send them home or I go home, and I ain't even met Sammy yet. I ain't done nothing yet. No TV shows lined up for us — I aint got none of that yet.

Then I came to find out, adding insult to injury, Richard had been sneaking back over to the West Side with Bob Bailey and them. He had been playing over there with those guys, and we didn't even know it. That is why he was missing the rehearsals. Esther had taken him over there, and Bob wanted to use Richard as his guitar player and had promised Richard a whole gang of things if he agreed to come over there. That was why he was so insistent upon that he didn't need anybody.

No, that really was like the last straw for me. So, I told Sonny, "I'm through with that. If you want to send them home, then send them." I'm done trying to beg him to give us one more chance as a group because I was still tryna keep us together. So, Sonny just cleans his hand of them, and before you know, that shit fell apart. Richard fell apart over on the West Side. The girl ran back off to her boyfriend or something. Paul went home. He finally got enough money to go get his car and he went home. Bobby went back home, and eventually Richard went back home.

There was just me and Sonny, that's when the adventure really started.

After the band disbursed and went back to St. Louis, I became just a little more depressed. Sonny could tell it — he would always try to find something for us to go out and tell it. I was steady thinkin' in my mind that I had failed. All the effort I put into this and I knew I would be better with the band, I left my wife, I got rid of all my assets, my son is getting older, my mom's on my back, and the band was breakin' apart.

Sonny's career was goin' down the drain, people was approachin' Sonny with lame kind of contracts and he could never read them, I would snatch the contract and say, "Let me see this contract... I never seen anything like this," and I would read it out, word for. He finally caught on that I knew he couldn't read that well. So I would do that so he could find out what they were talking about, and he began to trust me more and more. He depends on me for things like that.

Some of the little shysters would get upset because they knew if they could get by himself they might be able to slide something under him. He was smart enough to keep some lawyers around him to take care of his business, and discuss things with Geraldine. But on the spot, I was always there to protect him. He felt like he had a friend that he could have confidence in, that did have his best interest at heart. So he started bending over backwards to try and help me do things in order to keep me happy.

One day we went by the Stardust Hotel and they were having a big party over there. There was a bunch of dignitaries over there, he introduced me to Ted Turner and a guy named Kurt Cacoya. They had just built a hotel called the International Hilton Hotel on Paradise. It was the newest place in town and everybody was going there, and I spotted Kurt's wife. Boy, she was like drop dead gorgeous, I ain't never seen no titty implants before. She had some boobs that was stuck out to the moon, and had a great big ol' huge diamond danglin' in between them – about as big as a thumb – and I asked Sonny.

"Man, look at that foxy, see." He said.

"Yeah, that's Kurt's wife, they stay right down the street from me on the golf course, I see them everyday when I jog around." I was just mesmerized by this lady. Man, I was still a country boy. There was just so much going on, I got a chance to meet some more of those gangsters that Sonny knew. He introduced [me] to everybody and by then people were thinkin' that I was his son. Just assuming that because we were so close and was laughin' with each other all the time. They invited us to the Hilton — that was the first time that I walked in there. Man, the lights were dazzling and people were going in and out. They were talkin' about bringing Elvis Presley to the Hilton Hotel.

Elvis had been on a down spiral in his career at that time; they were trying to build him back up. Muhammad Ali was about to get back reinstated, and have a fight with Jerry Qaury at the Sedic's Center. Ike Turner was on his way there, and Redd Foxx.

The first time I met Redd Foxx, he was the lounge act at the Hilton Hotel, alternating with Wayne Crockren and the CC Ratter's. Man, I couldn't believe it was the same Redd Foxx from St. Louis and he had his own key in the window. Nobody could come in that window; they had it specially saved for Redd Foxx, and he was crazy about Sonny because Redd was a fight fanatic. He had a few fighters and everything else and then another thing, Redd was from St. Louis just like Sonny and me was. So Sonny introduced me to Redd and man, I was just flabbergasted cause' my folks had a lot of Redd Foxx albums. They used to make me go to bed and wouldn't let me hear 'em when I was a little guy.

All of a sudden there I am with Redd Foxx, man, and he just liked me just from the very beginning. Cause' I guess I was just representing St. Louis in the right manner, he used to say, "Hey! Little St. Louis, what's happenin'?" And I was so happy to be around Redd, I just could feel the home spirit in Redd.

Sonny would always tell me if you need to contact him to find me... Redd invited us to the show. I got to see the show for the first time and man, I must have laughed myself into a frenzy because he was so funny. This was before he had Cotton Comes to Harlem, Sanford & Son. None of this was going on. Redd had a manager named Bardu Allah. Bardu Allah used to come to Sonny all the time, asking if he would help Redd do some things, like get on Ed Sullivan or help him do some promotion. Because Sonny was still formerly the heavyweight champion of the world. Everybody knew Sonny Liston.

Redd at that time was climbing up the ladder and he was on his way. He was packing up that showroom, night after night, we was hanging out at that Hilton everyday. We started to callin' it an office. I was still staying over at that apartment that Sonny had gave me. I was lonesome over there man, I didn't have anybody but me over there, man. When it was time to go home, I'd feel so sad cause' I was thinkin' about my wife and kid, I just could never shake that. Sonny would come and pick me up every day and take me to the Hilton, or have me meet him, and I'd walk over there from the Stardust. We'd page each other to let us know that we were there.

Sonny would say, "Paging Charles Sonny Liston, paging Charles Sonny Liston!" And I would say, "Paging Gene Anderson, paging Gene Anderson!" They'd say it on the microphone and we would know that each of us was probably at the hotel. We had a certain section that we would meet up in, and Sonny would meet all kinds of stars that would come up in there. He had a plan he was going to try and build the first

Black hotel in Las Vegas. So he was gettin' the phone numbers to all of the Black stars that was coming into town, that was hanging out at the Hilton as well as those that was at different hotels.

One day we was walking through the hotel and we spotted Jerry Butler at the crap table. Jerry Butler at the time was smokin' hot; he had a record called *I Dig You Baby*. Sonny got down on his knees and sneaked up under the crap table. Took his keys, tapped him on the foot and jumped back real quick, Jerry was lookin' around. He sneaked over there and tapped him again and Jerry was looking around, he could never find 'em. All of a sudden he jumped up and said, "Boo!" and he scared the shit out of Jerry. He dropped the chips all over the floor. It was funnier than funny — we was down there trying to get the man's money up off the floor. He was so happy to see Sonny, they just hugged like two ol' school girls.

After Jerry got all his money accumulated off the floor we went over to sit down and had some cocktails. Over by the slot machines, Sonny told him about his idea for all of the Black stars getting together — how he could get the hook up and match the money and they could open up their own casino. At that time, that was a light year from becoming a reality because Blacks wasn't handling that much as they are today. Not only that but it was still the fabrics of Jim Crow was alive and well. They weren't letting Blacks do a lot of things and all these guys were pioneers breaking through the racial systems that was there to keep us out of things. Sonny was a very much in the forefront of Black entrepreneurship tryin' to get things moving for his people.

A lot of people were kinda listening to Sonny, and a lot of White guys I could hear under their breath would murmur, "That the nigger's were trying to get something going" to that effect, and I knew that they didn't really want Sonny to have that kind of power. But Sonny was smart. Sonny had a lot of things about him that people never really gave Sonny credit for. Because Sonny had quite a vision. Matter-a-fact, Sonny bought so many acres of Paradise Road coming from Deserts End, all the way up to probably Harmen — all that area there was all sand and cactus. Ah man, there wasn't nothing up there, right now it's the most premium real estate in Las Vegas. They got the Hardrock up there, big businesses, post offices, and huge apartment complexes.

But then it was just straight desert, and I asked Sonny why would you pay all that money for it? I think he paid like ten thousand or better for it, all this, it ain't nothin' but cactus and scorpions out here. He said. "Geney baby, let me tell you something, this town is growing and it's going to grow big, I'm going to own the prime real estate right here in the heart of Las Vegas and you'll see. One day this property is going to be really worth a lot of money." I couldn't understand it at that time, but as I look back today. I could see he was quite a visionary, because that property today is worth billions, not millions. He only paid ten thousand dollars for it, as I understand after he died.

The mob or whoever, they pressed Geraldine into giving it to them, because they said Sonny owed them some money. For that land and just straight took that from her and that just broke my heart when I found that out. Because that was Sonny's dream to use that part of Paradise Road to build that casino on. To get all the Blacks to get together, and rally behind him and get the money to build on the property he bought.

I felt really good about Sonny, Man, he would always introduce me to guys like Jerry Butler. That would make me feel like I was somebody he would present to them like I was so special. They would wonder who this little guy is with Sonny. Like one time we were walking down the strip and they had a merry-go-round. Going around some property over there somewhere by the Stardust. A film crew from Hollywood was filming a movie which I think was *The Grasshopper*, and there was Jim Brown, going around and around on this merry-go-round, and he saw Sonny and just broke character. "Sonny Boy! Sonny Boy!" Sonny saw him and they got to talkin', they shut down the whole film production to talk to each other.

Jim Brown was that kind of brother, he was a real honest-to-God, true brother that was hardcore for his people. For dignity, especially during those days, he was one of the earliest Black movie stars. During the

Blaxploitation movies, he pulled in guys like Fred Williamson. He made it possible for guys like Richard Pryor and a whole bunch of other guys to get into the movie scene. By being such a huge hall of fame football player, he had just made that big epic movie; *One Hundred Rifles*. With Sophia Lauren, man, he was like number one, and the way he felt about Sonny you could see it. The way he looked up to Sonny, that I was with the right guy. Just thinkin' about meeting Jim Brown I'm taken back, I'm still this country boy that don't know nothin'. I'm like yeah! Yessir Mr. Brown, Yessir. I was an excited man, and Sonny could see it, he would die laughin'. He would tell Jim Brown, he said. "Man, look at Geney Boy! He can't believe it's you."

I was really blessed and I knew it. They made an appointment to get together after the shoot and have dinner. We met over at the restaurant and in the meantime there was a lot of people from St. Louis that came into town. Mr. Powell came and I was so glad to see Mr. Powell with his ol' gangster self. He brought with him the guy that owned the St. Louis August Newspaper, who was one of the people that helped Sonny get out of the penitentiary. He was an old, old man and he had married a young drop dead gorgeous Redbone wife. Everybody was trying to hit on her, Sonny never tried to hit on her though and I never did. But everybody in the place was trying to hit on her, and she was just as loose as a goose.

After the band disbursed and went back to St. Louis, I became just a little more depressed. Sonny could tell it — he would always try to find something for us to go out and tell it. I was steady thinkin' in my mind that I had failed. All the effort I put into this and I knew I would be better with the band, I left my wife, I got rid of all my assets, my son is getting older, my mom's on my back, and the band was breakin' apart.

Sonny's career was goin' down the drain, people was approachin' Sonny with lame kind of contracts and he could never read them, I would snatch the contract and say, "Let me see this contract... I never seen anything like this," and I would read it out, word for. He finally caught on that I knew he couldn't read that well. So I would do that so he could find out what they were talking about, and he began to trust me more and more. He depends on me for things like that.

Some of the little shysters would get upset because they knew if they could get by himself they might be able to slide something under him. He was smart enough to keep some lawyers around him to take care of his business, and discuss things with Geraldine. But on the spot, I was always there to protect him. He felt like he had a friend that he could have confidence in, that did have his best interest at heart. So he started bending over backwards to try and help me do things in order to keep me happy.

One day we went by the Stardust Hotel and they were having a big party over there. There was a bunch of dignitaries over there, he introduced me to Ted Turner and a guy named Kurt Cacoya. They had just built a hotel called the International Hilton Hotel on Paradise. It was the newest place in town and everybody was going there, and I spotted Kurt's wife. Boy, she was like drop dead gorgeous, I ain't never seen no titty implants before. She had some boobs that was stuck out to the moon, and had a great big ol' huge diamond danglin' in between them – about as big as a thumb – and I asked Sonny.

"Man, look at that foxy, see." He said.

"Yeah, that's Kurt's wife, they stay right down the street from me on the golf course, I see them everyday when I jog around." I was just mesmerized by this lady. Man, I was still a country boy. There was just so much going on, I got a chance to meet some more of those gangsters that Sonny knew. He introduced [me] to everybody and by then people were thinkin' that I was his son. Just assuming that because we were so close and was laughin' with each other all the time. They invited us to the Hilton — that was the first time that I walked in there. Man, the lights were dazzling and people were going in and out. They were talkin' about bringing Elvis Presley to the Hilton Hotel.

Elvis had been on a down spiral in his career at that time; they were trying to build him back up. Muhammad Ali was about to get back reinstated, and have a fight with Jerry Qaury at the Sedic's Center. Ike Turner was on his way there, and Redd Foxx.

The first time I met Redd Foxx, he was the lounge act at the Hilton Hotel, alternating with Wayne Crockren and the CC Ratter's. Man, I couldn't believe it was the same Redd Foxx from St. Louis and he had his own key in the window. Nobody could come in that window; they had it specially saved for Redd Foxx, and he was crazy about Sonny because Redd was a fight fanatic. He had a few fighters and everything else and then another thing, Redd was from St. Louis just like Sonny and me was. So Sonny introduced me to Redd and man, I was just flabbergasted cause' my folks had a lot of Redd Foxx albums. They used to make me go to bed and wouldn't let me hear 'em when I was a little guy.

All of a sudden there I am with Redd Foxx, man, and he just liked me just from the very beginning. Cause' I guess I was just representing St. Louis in the right manner, he used to say, "Hey! Little St. Louis, what's happenin'?" And I was so happy to be around Redd, I just could feel the home spirit in Redd.

Sonny would always tell me if you need to contact him to find me... Redd invited us to the show. I got to see the show for the first time and man, I must have laughed myself into a frenzy because he was so funny. This was before he had Cotton Comes to Harlem, Sanford & Son. None of this was going on. Redd had a manager named Bardu Allah. Bardu Allah used to come to Sonny all the time, asking if he would help Redd do some things, like get on Ed Sullivan or help him do some promotion. Because Sonny was still formerly the heavyweight champion of the world. Everybody knew Sonny Liston.

Redd at that time was climbing up the ladder and he was on his way. He was packing up that showroom, night after night, we was hanging out at that Hilton everyday. We started to callin' it an office. I was still staying over at that apartment that Sonny had gave me. I was lonesome over there man, I didn't have anybody but me over there, man. When it was time to go home, I'd feel so sad cause' I was thinkin' about my wife and kid, I just could never shake that. Sonny would come and pick me up every day and take me to the Hilton, or have me meet him, and I'd walk over there from the Stardust. We'd page each other to let us know that we were there.

Sonny would say, "Paging Charles Sonny Liston, paging Charles Sonny Liston!" And I would say, "Paging Gene Anderson, paging Gene Anderson!" They'd say it on the microphone and we would know that each of us was probably at the hotel. We had a certain section that we would meet up in, and Sonny would meet all kinds of stars that would come up in there. He had a plan he was going to try and build the first Black hotel in Las Vegas. So he was gettin' the phone numbers to all of the Black stars that was coming into town, that was hanging out at the Hilton as well as those that was at different hotels.

One day we was walking through the hotel and we spotted Jerry Butler at the crap table. Jerry Butler at the time was smokin' hot; he had a record called *I Dig You Baby*. Sonny got down on his knees and sneaked up under the crap table. Took his keys, tapped him on the foot and jumped back real quick, Jerry was lookin' around. He sneaked over there and tapped him again and Jerry was looking around, he could never find 'em. All of a sudden he jumped up and said, "Boo!" and he scared the shit out of Jerry. He dropped the chips all over the floor. It was funnier than funny — we was down there trying to get the man's money up off the floor. He was so happy to see Sonny, they just hugged like two ol' school girls.

After Jerry got all his money accumulated off the floor we went over to sit down and had some cocktails. Over by the slot machines, Sonny told him about his idea for all of the Black stars getting together — how he could get the hook up and match the money and they could open up their own casino. At that time, that was a light year from becoming a reality because Blacks wasn't handling that much as they are today. Not only that but it was still the fabrics of Jim Crow was alive and well. They weren't letting Blacks do a lot of things and all these guys were pioneers breaking through the racial systems that was there to keep us out of things. Sonny was a very much in the forefront of Black entrepreneurship tryin' to get things moving for his people.

A lot of people were kinda listening to Sonny, and a lot of White guys I could hear under their breath would murmur, "That the nigger's were trying to get something going" to that effect, and I knew that they didn't really want Sonny to have that kind of power. But Sonny was smart. Sonny had a lot of things about him that people never really gave Sonny credit for. Because Sonny had quite a vision. Matter-a-fact, Sonny bought so many acres of Paradise Road coming from Deserts End, all the way up to probably Harmen — all that area there was all sand and cactus. Ah man, there wasn't nothing up there, right now it's the most premium real estate in Las Vegas. They got the Hardrock up there, big businesses, post offices, and huge apartment complexes.

But then it was just straight desert, and I asked Sonny why would you pay all that money for it? I think he paid like ten thousand or better for it, all this, it ain't nothin' but cactus and scorpions out here. He said. "Geney baby, let me tell you something, this town is growing and it's going to grow big, I'm going to own the prime real estate right here in the heart of Las Vegas and you'll see. One day this property is going to be really worth a lot of money." I couldn't understand it at that time, but as I look back today. I could see he was quite a visionary, because that property today is worth billions, not millions. He only paid ten thousand dollars for it, as I understand after he died.

The mob or whoever, they pressed Geraldine into giving it to them, because they said Sonny owed them some money. For that land and just straight took that from her and that just broke my heart when I found that out. Because that was Sonny's dream to use that part of Paradise Road to build that casino on. To get all the Blacks to get together, and rally behind him and get the money to build on the property he bought.

I felt really good about Sonny, Man, he would always introduce me to guys like Jerry Butler. That would make me feel like I was somebody he would present to them like I was so special. They would wonder who this little guy is with Sonny. Like one time we were walking down the strip and they had a merry-go-round. Going around some property over there somewhere by the Stardust. A film crew from Hollywood was filming a movie which I think was *The Grasshopper*, and there was Jim Brown, going around and around on this merry-go-round, and he saw Sonny and just broke character. "Sonny Boy! Sonny Boy!" Sonny saw him and they got to talkin', they shut down the whole film production to talk to each other.

Jim Brown was that kind of brother, he was a real honest-to-God, true brother that was hardcore for his people. For dignity, especially during those days, he was one of the earliest Black movie stars. During the Blaxploitation movies, he pulled in guys like Fred Williamson. He made it possible for guys like Richard Pryor and a whole bunch of other guys to get into the movie scene. By being such a huge hall of fame football player, he had just made that big epic movie; *One Hundred Rifles*. With Sophia Lauren, man, he was like number one, and the way he felt about Sonny you could see it. The way he looked up to Sonny, that I was with the right guy. Just thinkin' about meeting Jim Brown I'm taken back, I'm still this country boy that don't know nothin'. I'm like yeah! Yessir Mr. Brown, Yessir. I was an excited man, and Sonny could see it, he would die laughin'. He would tell Jim Brown, he said. "Man, look at Geney Boy! He can't believe it's you."

I was really blessed and I knew it. They made an appointment to get together after the shoot and have dinner. We met over at the restaurant and in the meantime there was a lot of people from St. Louis that came into town. Mr. Powell came and I was so glad to see Mr. Powell with his ol' gangster self. He brought with him the guy that owned the St. Louis August Newspaper, who was one of the people that helped Sonny get out of the penitentiary. He was an old, old man and he had married a young drop dead gorgeous Redbone wife. Everybody was trying to hit on her, Sonny never tried to hit on her though and I never did. But everybody in the place was trying to hit on her, and she was just as loose as a goose.

Sonny's Story

We got into the car, headed across the desert on I-15, headed to Los Angeles. Hollywood, man — I was finally gonna get there.

I was so excited, I didn't know how to respond. I didn't want to let Sonny know that my heart was beating so fast at the thought that this was gonna be my great big chance. He was so influenced by the thought that he was gonna get that money. Sonny had a new career coming with this new record, all the connections he had and all the promises he made me. I was gonna get a chance to ride along with him. He played the cassette in the car over and over again, as we rode down the highway. We were singing our ass off. I've never seen Sonny so happy.

Cassettes were king in those days and man we was playing it and rolling. We were almost to Barstow, and the cassette got caught up in the player. He tried getting it out, it unraveled and man he almost had a heart attack. He frowned, screamed, and hollered. He couldn't be mad at no one but himself, because he was operating it. I couldn't explain that these things happen like that, because he didn't know that much about that kind of technology. Sonny was a fighter. He didn't know how things malfunctioned and stuff, all he knew was the damn song was torn up and we hadn't got to California yet. He didn't know that I had an extra cassette with me in my pocket, so I went into my pocket and pulled out the extra cassette.

Just so happened he didn't know what to do, if he was a little gay, he would've kissed me. That was my friend man, he wouldn't play it no more in the car, no more chances.

This is the true Sonny Liston. He would tell me things. It's hard right now for me to even try to reveal everything because it's a lot of personal stuff.

First thing I asked him was how he ended up fighting in the beginning. He said, "Man, I had a real rough childhood and my folks, there was so many of us and my daddy was such a cruel person." And he used to beat him all the time, which made him mad at everyone. He ran away from home about twelve years old from Sand Slough, Arkansas to St. Louis to try to find his mother. He didn't know anybody in St. Louis. He had some nerve to be a youngster like that and scuffle up a few pennies, get on a greyhound bus and go all the way to St. Louis by himself. He didn't know what his future was gonna hold, but he knew staying down wasn't going to work. He always tried to better himself.

So, he finally got into school but that didn't work for him either. He was so much bigger than everyone else in grammar school they used to laugh and tease him. The type of person that he was, he would just start to fight them and kick they ass. Them young boys couldn't hurt him. In his heart he really didn't want to hurt nobody, so he just dropped out of school, didn't go any more. He just roamed around St. Louis and running into all kinds of street guys and started meeting girls and stuff.

He started strong-arming people because he couldn't read or write. It was back in Jim Crow days and everything else. He wasn't in a position to do no honest labor, and they wasn't hiring Blacks hardly for nothing. He didn't have any education as we all knew, he just did what the streets opened up for his life. So, he began to stick up people, run around with the wrong guys, and just make money in the streets.

He started getting new shoes, new suits, meeting girls, and he began to like the finer things in life. Sonny always was attracted by beautiful and wonderful things by him thirsting for it as a kid growing up. He was finding his way to get to the fortune of life that he somehow craved for.

He met some gangsters and was a strong arm for them. When he was a teenager, he was as big as a grown man. He would collect money for them. They had jukeboxes in different places. One place had a jukebox, and the guy wasn't making no money with it, so he personally picked the jukebox up, took it out the store and set it out on the curb. Then he set it on a truck and took it from the guy. He said he used to beat up guys as a strap breaker or something like that.

He was telling me how he used to collect money for the mob. There was a thing called shylocking. They would get a huge percentage over the amount they loaned in a certain amount of time. If they were late on the payment, he would just kick their ass and break their legs for the mob. As time went on his name got around the underground circuit. He became the Black Hand. Everybody wanted Sonny to do their dirty work for them, even boys up in Kanas City was asking him to do their dirty work for them. So, he began to be quite a name for those gangsters, and he had courage to do all kinds of things.

This is how he went to jail. He said that he was sticking up people and the police in St. Louis was consistently harassing him every chance they got. Sometimes the police would call him a nigger and beat him down. He was really strong, so it made the police hate him in those days. Then one day he robbed someone, and they busted him, locked him up in the penitentiary.

While he was in the penitentiary, he was so frustrated about being locked up because he felt that he never got a good chance. He would come out of the cell and see someone he didn't like, just walk up to him and knock him out cold. They put him in the hole. It didn't make no difference if he fought or knocked him out cold. He would get back out of the hole and see some big guys picking on some little guys. He always was a champion for the little guy and got in the middle and started fighting them.

One day the warden asked him, "Sonny, why is that you always fighting. Listen, why don't you just calm down and just consider fighting for us. WE need a champion."

Sonny looked at him and said, "I don't see why not. I ain't doin' nothing no way except rotting away in here. I tell you what, I'll make you a deal. If you get me some whiskey, every now and then get me a girl, I'll fight for you."

He thought they would never fall for that, but somehow the warden said, "Okay, if you win for us, you got it."

So, he started to train in the penitentiary and started having fights. The first fight or two he won and knocked a guy out. Before you know it wasn't nobody left to fight. He knocked everybody out in the penitentiary, except a few guys who went the distance. But he beat them down so bad that they started to send him to different penitentiaries to fight all over the state. He became the heavyweight champion.

Father Alois Stevenson was his mentor, the only one he really trusted. The warden, the St. Louis Star newspaper, and Senator John F. Kennedy became aware.

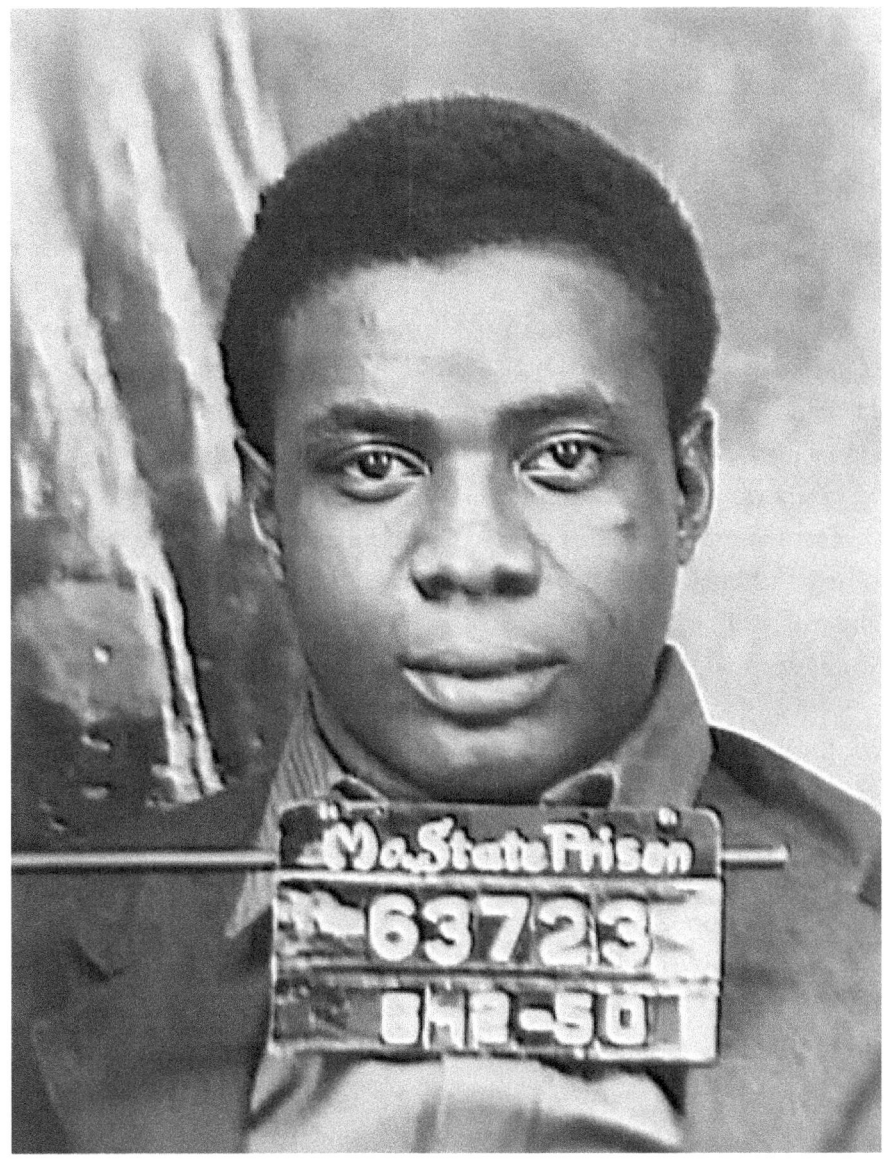

Hollywood Road Trip

A few days after he came by the hotel, he said."Geney Boy let's go." I said. "Let's go where Sonny?" I done forgotten all about it... He said. "Let's go see Sammy my mind up. We finna go see Sammy man, Imma introduce him to you and we gon' make something happen. Matter-a-fact we gon' hook up some TV shows and everything else for you."

I was so excited we just danced around like we was boogie with each other, and boxin' around. Cause' Sonny used to like to do that rough and tuff stuff wit me, and I used to like it because I was a tuff little youngster myself. So I looked at him, man, his was sharp, he had on a black Moorad suit with red pinstripes, with black shiny alligator shoes on, he didn't have a hat on this time, man he looked like... he was as fresh as a daisy. Man, he done cleaned his act up from the party that we had done out in Hollywood.

I knew we were on our way, we had got in the car en route out of town. We stopped by the last liquor store, which I knew was not going to be a pleasure ride from then on out. But I couldn't stop him — he bought a fifth of Smirnoff Vodka. He took the cap off of it and drank down at least about an eighth of it in one big swallow. Snapped his finger and swipe his mouth, "Ahhhh!" Before you know it that's when I found out that an alcoholic don't take a whole lot to really get em drunk. He was drunk like he took a half a gallon. I couldn't believe it, then he said let's turn the car around. We had gotten at least on the outskirts out of town, we was bout five or six miles outside of Las Vegas. He made me get off at the next ramp turn around and go back to the Stardust, to see if we could find this little blonde girl, Connie Shaw.

I didn't too much mind to be truthful, but I really wanted to get on down the road cause' I knew that this was our chance. But she was so fine, boy, as I said she was gorgeous, she was so young and pretty. I knew that I had a shot with her, I thought that maybe I would be able to carry and steal her from this boy sho'. I had on a long run like this one, so I was glad to make that U-turn and went back down there to Stardust over at the hooker nook, and there she was just as gorgeous as ever. When she saw me she was kinda glad to see me, we was about the same age. I was nice to her but she didn't want to see Sonny.

I said."Come on baby, Sonny wants to see you and make up for the last time..."

She said, "No, I don't know if I want to deal with Sonny."

And I just begged and pleaded. "Come on now, you know how he is. He won't let me rest until he can make it up to you. Some days he's okay and some days he ain't, but today he's ok." I just talked to her and talked to her.

And she said, "Well, I'll come out there and talk to him for a little while, but I'm not going nowhere wit ya'll."

So I got her to the car and when he saw her, his face just lit up. He has gotten to the back seat of the car, and I opened the door for her. She saw him and she had just a little small trembling look on her face. But she wasn't really scared of Sonny because she knew she was safe in the parking lot. All she had to do was just jump out the car or don't get in the car. So she took the choice and got in the car, he spoke to her; I could see in his face that he was drunk already. The Vodka done kicked in, he looked at me and gave her that stare and he told me. "Drive off Geney Boy."

She tried to get out the car. He grabbed her by the head and snatched her back in the car, slammed the door, and I took off, because if he said it, I did it. I took off and then he kinda like jacked her up.

"Sonny Boy, let me out the car."

"Bitch I ain't letting you go nowhere."

So, she know how he is, the next thing for her to do was to negotiate for the money. She said. "If I'm goin' to go party with y'all, you gotta pay me in advance — give me some money now."

Sonny asked her what she wanted. She asked for a hundred; he went in his pocket and gave her a hundred-dollar bill. We took off across the highway, down the 15 fly. It was late, hardly cars on the highway. He grabbed her, made her give him some head down the highway: one time, two time, three times. Boy I was laughin' my ass off because he would be makin' funny faces laughin' at me. Poking me up besides my head while I was driving just so I could go back and look at 'em. He died laughin' cause he was a clown wit that kinda shit.

He done got good at drunk by now, so we was rollin' and some weed in her purse. She done kicked back by now, she got the little money. She don't know where she going, she figure we just riding around the highway. Probably take her to the hotel, fuck her real good, and then bring her back. Because she knew how Sonny was and she had already put herself in the position where she made some money. And when she come back with that little money, she can go back to Charles Shaw, tell 'em that she was with Sonny, what the deal was, and let 'em deal with Sonny. So she was kinda like kick back cool for a minute.

So he just insisted that I pull the car over. I wonder what he wanted. He said. "You get in the backseat, and let this bitch give you some head too."

I said. "Sonny, I'm kinda like hung up about that." 'Cause I didn't know how he gon to respond because Sonny was so hot n' cold so quick. But I knew that he always wanted me to enjoy whatever he felt he was enjoying. I pulls the car over, I get back in the backseat, and she give me some head. He stick his hand all up under her dress, boy we just doggin' this little girl out. And she lovin' it.

I don't understand the mentality of a hoe to this day. Everything they say they don't want is what they did want. She just begin to have fun and smoke, tootin' cocaine with us, and it was okay. We freakin' out on the goddamn highway — it don't make no sense to me now. But back then I guess it was the thang to do 'cause I was young as ever. Sonny was just as wild and crazy as I was to be truthful, he might have been older, but he was just as young as I was. Because sometimes he mentality was a straight teenager and other times was as serious as a heart attack. Never knew how he was gonna come hot or cold, it didn't matter to me. I knew I could deal with Sonny however he came, I knew in my heart that he knew I really loved him, like a big brother or father figure. Sooner or later he would come back around and straighten up with me. He would never go too far with me, but you could never know about Sonny.

I get back to the driver seat and we start heading back to 15 towards Hollywood. We go up on this ramp where it's midway [between] Nevada and Los Angeles, where they have an inspection for produce on the 15, and we went through the inspection. No one luckily was in the booth and we just drove right on through. But right on the other side of this inspection station was some little small bungalow hotels Sonny knew about. He had me to pull off the road and into a little dirt road and there they were. It was closed down because it was late at night. It was about five or six little bungalow's and a main office, so I pulled into the main office area. I parked the car, Sonny told me to go get the room, I get out the car knock on the door.

An old White man comes to the door he lookin' like he ain't seen a Black person in his life. But he looked at me and he looked at the Cadillac, but he couldn't see in the windows. He asked me did I want a room, what am I doin', he askin' me a bunch of questions. Really trying to get into my business and he's perturbed because I woke 'em up at the time of night. I told him I wanted a room for me and my uncle, something like that. We was in the car and we were traveling and we want to get a room. He charged me the little 35 or 25 dollars, whatever it was.

But anyway, I fill out the application and got the key and gave it to Sonny. Sonny drove the car to the suite number on the key. I was getting the change from the man, and for him to give us a 10 o'clock wake-up call. At that same moment, Sonny gets out the car and got that girl by the head. She's screamin' "Ow! Ow!", throws her in the door and slams the door hard. I'm still in the lobby with the man. The man said. "What the hell is going on here?"

I clammed up and said. "Man, I don't know what's going on."

I just got my change and rushed over to the bungalow. I go into the bungalow, the broad had did something to piss em off, and he jacked her up. That's why she was screaming in the room. I said. "Sonny, what to think?"

He said, "Fuck 'em, we gon party wit this bitch, and we gon stay here until tomorrow." So we all took our clothes off and we freaked out. I freaked her, he freaked her, she we into her purse, pulled out a vibrator and freaked herself. We just smoked weed and tooted cocaine, and drank that vodka. We were just partying, three of us sitting there playing cards, all of a sudden we had been there at least three hours or so.

It was still dark outside and we heard something beat on the door. It was a real hard knock like a big stick or something, Sonny say, "Answer the door." She jumps up, grabs a sheet, puts it around herself and ran in the back room, got in the shower, and pulled the shower curtain, cause she knew she was a hoe. She probably had warrants and everything else and she wasn't trying to really gets us in trouble. She was just trying to protect herself and hide in the shower on her own. I'm naked, Sonny naked, Sonny gets behind the door. The door is like a platform step up and we got the chain on the door. He whispers, "Answer the door."

I say, "Who is it?" My voice is just as high as Micheal Jackson.

He say, "It's the Sheriff goddamn it."

I say, "The Sheriff."

He said," Yeah, it's the Sheriff and I heard you got a White woman there again' her will."

I started to thinkin', oh shit, oh man I'm in trouble right now, my wife gon' find out about this. It's gon hit the press. We took this bitch across the state lines, and she, a young girl, White woman and the Sheriff outside, they done seen Sonny throw this woman in the room. Two

Black guys, this one White girl. All this is flashing into my mind, in less than a half of a millimeter of a second.

He say, "Open this goddamn door!"

So I crack the door and he sees me half naked. He didn't see all of me. But he sees a Black youngster and he knows he's about to have a field day kickin' my ass. Cause' the old man done already called him up and told him that two niggas got the White woman in there and it seems like it's against her will.

He says to me, "Yeah I hear you nigger boys got some White gal in here again' her will, open this goddamn door."

Sonny signals me, open the door, open the door. I pushed the door closed a little bit, slid the chain off it. And he bust through the door like gangbusters. He lookin' like John Wayne standing up there over me. He said. "Where's that white woman?"

All of a sudden Sonny slams the door behind em, Sonny grabs him by the collar, picks him up off the floor, and takes his gun out of the holster in the same movement – just like that – and slam his head up against the wall. He beats his head up against the wall about four or five times.

I'm pulling on Sonny, saying, "Sonny, please, it's the police, don't do it!" and he beat him up side the head.

And Sonny say, "Yeah motherfucker, we two freaks, we freakin' off and you done disturbed us."

He looked at Sonny and say, "Goddamn, Sonny Liston!"

Boy I thought I would die laughin'. Sonny threw him down on the floor. We both stand there, butthole naked, and the dude say, "Sonny man, if I had known it was you, Sonny Boy, I never would have came here. The man just told me that there were some Black guys that had a White girl hostage. I never would have came by here. Just give me my gun, man. I'm the chief of police. Just give me my gun, man, and I'll go up about my business."

Sonny opened the door and threw him out of the door — I mean handled him like a ragdoll. Threw out there on the dirt, took his gun and threw it out there in the pitch black desert. He kicked him in the ass wit his barefoot and told 'em to get the fuck outta there and don't come back until he leaves this town.

The dude got in his car, I'm shaking like a motherfucker... I shakin' like a sail in the wind. He gets in his car and he speeds off. Rocks fly off and he spins rubber getting away from there. Sonny throws bricks – gravel rather – all on the back of the man's car, butthole naked. I'm laughin my ass off, I can't believe this is happening. So we rush back in the door, I got to thinkin', well shit, I got to pack our shit, we got to get the fuck up outta here. I started to pack the clothes and get my clothes on...

Sonny said. "Wait a minute Geney Boy, what the fuck you doing?"

I said, " Sonny man, this motherfucker gon' come back with an army of police."

He said, "Fuck 'em! Get your clothes off, bitch come out that toilet." He went in there and snatched the shower curtains off the hooks. He threw them on the floor and said. "Bitch get up outta here!" She came out. "Suck my dick again, bitch." He made the bitch suck his dick again, I fucked her and he fucked her again. We played cards and started to tootin' cocaine like nothin' ever happened.

So, sometime within that night we all finally laid down and went to sleep. She gets up out the bed wit Sonny, sneaks over there with me. She sticks her head up under the cover and gives me some head, then goes to sleep in my arms, and the next morning the sun is just as bright. It must have been eight or nine o' clock in the morning, and Sonny snatches her up out the bed.

He drank again – he was still drinking that shit – and he picked me up, and he pops me in the nose. He said, "Whatcha doin' wit my bitch?" Real light, a love tap, it wasn't no bang! It was just a little love tap. Boy I hit em up besides his head about five or six times. He burst out, and got to covering up like a little sissy. He started laughin' his ass off, I mean he was on the floor rollin'. He say, "You little mother fucker, you say, you'll fight, won't you? I'm just bullshittin' wit you!"

I said, "Man, I'm just bullshittin' wit you too, but don't you hit me no mother fuckin mo." And boy he just loved that. Man, we laughed so much about that. So we just fucked her again, and she didn't get ready fast enough. We started packing the car, she still fuckin' around tootin' that cocaine, because we had a gang of it. He grabs her head and threw a sheet around her. Now she's naked and threw her ass in the car done left her clothes. I pull off in the car, he made me drive off and took off down the highway.

Now here's a young White girl with no clothes on, with a toga sheet wrapped around her. We were headin' down the highway to Hollywood, on the way to see Sammy Davis, Jr. — so I thought. We rode a little bit longer and the next thing I know we went through a little town called Bakersville. Sonny knows some old gangsters that owns some old nightclubs down there in Bakersville. He wants to see them, so we roll through the town.

Until we come up to this little nightclub, I couldn't think of the name of the club. It was... it sort of like an after-hours joint. It had been open all night and it was still customers partying from last night. They had strippers and everything in this little joint, it was a gangster club. When we walked through the door, he got this girl, she got the sheet wrapped around her still. He has her by the head, he is still holding her and she is bent over like a hunchback. His hand is at the top of her head, dragging this young White girl, and the bar was all the way at the other end of the club. It was a nice little ways from the font door to the bar, and there were tables in between.

Sonny comes in there and kicks the door open just like Liberty Balance or somebody. I mean he was like the bull in the china store, he ain't sharp like he was at first. His clothes is all crazy and that pretty suit he got the coat buttoned up wrong. I'm right there with 'em just like Lone Ranger and Tonto. I'm right there with 'em, and when he kicks the door, he kicked it so hard everybody turned their attention to the door. You heard people murmur 'Sonny Liston', 'Sonny Liston', 'That's Sonny Liston'.

So he walks, trying to focus his eyes — he's fucked up. He walks through the tables headed towards the bar. He's taking people's drinks as he goes and drinking them down, wasting it all over himself. He must of did it to about four or five different tables. He steadily got this White girl and people looking at him. Women are appalled, he's acting a fool, and I'm walkin' around like fuck 'me, I'm with Sonny. By the time we came up to the bar he done took about five or six drinks. People were upset with him and some people were leaving.

The bartender walked up to him, and he knew who he was. He also knew that Sonny was a good friend with the boss, who was in the mob. So they couldn't just do something to Sonny, they was trying to pacify Sonny. Sonny was askin' for the guy and the guy wasn't there. He was raising so much hell and all of a sudden a little ol' lady – must of been about eighty-years old – she gets on a cane and walks up to Sonny, in front of everybody. She stuck her finger in his face and say, "You monster! You outta get here, what's wrong wit you? If I was just a little bit younger I would do something to you!"

Boy, when she said that I must have peed on myself laughing so hard. He looked down at her, she must have been about three feet, maybe four feet tall. He looked at her and he just died laughin'. He say – man, she is still looking up – and he says, "Geney Boy! We better get out of here before this here lady kick both of us in the ass."

And so he started taking people's drinks and drinking them. As we walked back out the door, and they were getting out of his way like he was a freight train. We got in the car and both of us started laughing, even the girl started laughin'. Even Connie Shaw started laughing and said, "That old lady was finna whoop our ass." We must of laugh about that all the way down the highway.

Not too long, about an hour or so we made our way to Los Angeles. Went down Wilshire Boulevard and we pulled up in front of the Ambassador Hotel, which Sammy Davis, Jr. owned a nightclub at the time called the Coconut Grove. When we pulled up in front of it, the doorman came to the car and he recognized Sonny. They got to chit-chatting and Sonny asked, "Is Sammy there? I came to see Sammy Davis."

He said, "Well, Mr. Davis just left. He should be back momentarily. Would you like to wait?"

Sonny agreed, so we pulled over to the curb, and we was going to sit and wait on Sammy. My mind got to clickin' I said man, "We can see Sammy a little later on man." Sonny done got all funky, his clothes all messed up. He got alcohol all over his outfit, I had been up all night. We got this naked White girl and Sonny is totally drunk. I didn't want to meet Sammy like that — I wanted to give him an impression of me in the right circumstances. But what I should have known was that Sammy was familiar with Sonny. He knew how Sonny acts and what Sonny would do. Who was I to try and categorize how Sonny should introduce me to Sammy Davis? Knowing that my greatest wish of the whole episode was to meet Sammy Davis. No, instead I convinced him to go to a hotel to freshen up and come back later on to meet Sammy.

That was the biggest mistake I ever made in my life because it never happened in that particular point in time. I always never forgave myself and I learned a big lesson about trying to make things so perfect. Instead of just taking it like it really came, it took a lot of more years later before I got a chance to meet and become a great friend/associate with Sammy Davis, Jr.. Sonny kind of agreed with me so we went across the street. From the Ambassador to another hotel, The Worshire Hide House — that was the name of the hotel at that time. That is where Sonny had lived, he told me, when he was champion. And that he always got the presidential suite, so I made the U-turn and went across the street.

We parked into the driveway and we got out of the car, people were looking at him. It was an aristocratic hotel and a lot of bougie people were there. We walked through the door just like Cotton Comes to Harlem. Okay, here we are, he still got this White girl by the head bent over, with the sheet wrapped around her. When we walks into the lobby, people started to look at us like 'What the fuck is this?' The manager knew exactly who he was. "Mr. Liston! Mr. Liston! Mr. Liston!"

Sonny staggers over there to the desk, and calls me up to the desk to fill out the paperwork for the room. He tells 'em he wants the presidential suite, where he had stayed when he was heavyweight champion of the world. He wanted the memories to be around, because he was still showing out for me. Which, I loved 'em for that, and he asked for the security guard, "Is the security guard around?" drunk as he could be.

So the manager of the hotel got on the intercom and he called for a security guard. A few minutes later, a young tall blonde-headed kid showed up. He's about thirty or thirty-five years old, muscle-bound, lookin' like another John Wayne I guess. He walks up to Sonny and says, "Yeah, what can I do for you?"

Sonny looked him up and down, and he grabbed 'em by the collar. He slammed him up against the counter and he took his pistol too. And he said, "I'm Sonny Boy Liston, and I'm going to be in this damn hotel a week or more. If I see your ass again, Imma kick yo ass. I don't never wanna see your face no more."

And everybody was lookin' at Sonny like 'Whoa!' Some of the customers looked like they was going to panic. He pushed the boy and damn near threw him down. The boy didn't say shit, Sonny put the gun back on the counter. The boy sneaked, like tiptoed, put his fingers up there. Put his gun in his pocket and broke and ran out the back door. Now what kind of security guard is that?

We got up on the elevator and he still got this girl by the head. Sonny threw her in the elevator and we went upstairs to the suite.

That was the first time I ever seen a presidential suite this was as big as a whole house. Man, when we first got off the elevator, there was a huge foyer and wall-to-wall couches. Plants were all over the place and we were so high up in the air that the clouds were coming up through the terrace doors. You could see the entire Hollywood up on the terrace and we went to the three of four big, huge bedrooms. We went to the toilet area — that was the first time I ever saw a dressing room for the toilet area. It was surrounded by mirrors and it had a big white carpet that was wall-to-wall. They had three different vase bowls,.

It was all so different. I'm still a country boy. I had never seen this. Sonny was looking at me laughing because he knew I was enjoying it. He said, "Geney Boy, you should've been there with me when I was champion." He always would say that when he would show me something that he knew was impressing me. To let me know that it had been better than that, and I was so favorable in his heart that. He loved when I could enjoy some of that as well. To this day, I still appreciate his love for me and the way that he tried to expose things to me. And I did learn a lot, see a lot with Sonny of those types of luxuries in life. Today I am able to enjoy and be a recipient of thanks to him. Sonny made sure that I could see as much as there was available. For me to be ready in life, when my turn came out here on my own.

So we settled down in the suite and he called a girlfriend of his, a Black lady. I can't remember her name but she was very close to Sonny. I remember meeting her once earlier in Las Vegas. He had taken her to dinner and stuff, she was one of his old girlfriends, who was truly one of his consistent lovers. She lived in Los Angeles. She was a very respectable woman — I think she was a school teacher, politician, or something. But anyway, she knew Sonny and how he was. She was one of the few people that could discipline Sonny, where he would calm down. The one reason I remember her so well is because the only well-taken photograph that I have with Sonny was with him, her, and myself. We were at the Landmark Hotel, I remember because he called me over to the booth to take a picture with em. I don't know what happened to the photo 'cause I never seen it anymore. I'm sure she does have it, I can't think of her name...

But nevertheless, she came over to the hotel. Sonny laid out a seafood feast for her. Now if that wasn't the first time I'd ever since a seafood platter; with oysters, shrimp, crab and lobster all that on ice. They brought that to the room, and I had a big problem eating raw oysters. Sonny was just eating them and pouring the lemon juice on them. Trying to make me eat 'em, boy, he's wrestling on the bed with me trying to make me eat them. I was fight 'em back. Boy, we was having the time of our life.

She kept watching the little White girl, she couldn't understand why she didn't have no clothes. Sonny was steadily telling her that she was my girlfriend. She was on my ass about the girl up in the sheet. I was trying to lie and tell her that well, she was a little hippie girl. This is the way they wear clothes, explaining it was a toga. She looked at me like 'boy, you better stop lying to me'. I'm trying to make up all kinds of stories that I can.

So, she decided to take Sonny and I to a nightclub in Hollywood. We showed up at the club. Man, it was jumping. Everything was going on. Girls in mini skirts, the players was there, the bands was playing. When we came up in there everybody just froze 'cause Sonny Liston was breathtaking. You saw him, you knew there was going to be about one or two things. He was going to spend a lot of money and be the life of the party or he was going to be a straight havoc. He was going to rock this joint and tear it all apart.

That's when I met this guy named Manzel. Manzel was a pimp and he hung out with the top players in Hollywood. He was a dope man; he took Sonny and I to the side. He hit us with drugs once or twice — cocaine that was so strong that I just cried like a baby, and Sonny loved it. Sonny was like, "Man, where'd you get this from?"

He was like, "I got it."

Sonny said, "Well listen, come on over to the hotel and let's sit down and talk."

We party for a little bit afterwards. We made our way towards the hotel. After we got off the elevator, I started to look for Connie, the little White girl. I looked all around the room. She wasn't there. I wondered where she was. So I went downstairs and I asked the people at the front desk had they seen her, they said yeah, she left shortly after we did. I couldn't understand where she was going to go, she didn't have no clothes not nothing. I figured well maybe she went down to the store somewhere, maybe she turned a trick to get her some money, so she could get home or whatever it was. I did not know what the situation was. Sonny was kinda worried about her because she had become one of the fellas. She had been with us so long on this ride, he was used to having her around. She was beginning to look like she was enjoying herself, even though she had been run through the mill. She was laughing and partying and getting high with us. Playing cards and talking, the whole nine yards!

Next thing I knew about five o'clock that morning Manzel shows up. We around the table and we start to tootin', he pulls out a rock about as big as a golf ball. I've never seen that before. I say, "Sonny what's that?" And he took a little off and started scraping dust off. I still didn't know what it was. I repeated, "Sonny what's that?"

Sonny started laughin'. He said, "It's cocaine, man."

I ain't never seen no cocaine come in a great big ball like that. What it was, it was pure cocaine. It was in a big solid rock, a hard rock fashion. I tried to toot it, it was just too damn hot. It was burning my face off, I couldn't do nothing with it, man. Sonny was laughing his ass off. Sonny bought about fifteen-hundred dollars' worth of it.

Manzel went on home and we finally went to sleep. The next day about seven or eight o'clock in the morning, we get a phone call. It's Connie — she calls to let me know that she done made it all the way back to Las Vegas. She done hitchhiked with no shoes and just a sheet around her. All the way back to Las Vegas, and turned a trick. She was giving us the stink finger talking 'bout see you suckers later. She died laughing and then hung up in my face. I couldn't wait to tell Sonny.

Sonny say, "The little bitch." He was relieved that she done made it all the way back home. But he knew that she had problems with that pimp. 'Cause he was a fool, we knew 'me – Charles Shaw – we knew 'em. She done run off with us as far as he was concerned, and boy was he giving her the blues. But nevertheless she was okay and we had another day hanging out.

Now we started doing something called jailing. We were hanging around the hotel 'cause he thought we were broke. We didn't have no money, we spent all our money, we was waiting to see if we could get a few dollars from here or there. But in the meantime, we was cooling out playin' Cooncan [card game]. I knew all the time that we had money, because I was handling all the money since we left Vegas. I had a sock full of hundred-dollar bills, but I wasn't going to give the money to Sonny or let him know. Because earlier on in the game, Sonny was spending too much money too fast. I knew that he needed someone to keep a little discipline on him so I acted like I was broke. As far as he was concerned, I was broke, so I sat there, I began to come to and become sober. He started to looking better and eat like we were supposed to be. We already put enough money on the books to have the hotel room taken care of for a week anyway.

So we started playing Cooncan and jailing like I said. Jailing is when you can't go nowhere, you're sitting in a cell more-less. But the room and you just sit there and get your plans together. Nobody knows where you're at and you don't know where nobody is. It don't matter your just coolin' out — that's what we used to call jailing. In the process of it all he was trying to teach me a really strong lesson about something. We were clowning each other and we got down to the last few cards on the deck. I'm waiting on him to go, he throws down an ace. Oh! That's what I've been waiting on, I had two, three, a four. An ace made my hand — bam! Coon on his ass. So I started getting up laughing and dancing, I said. "Ok, Sonny, give me those cards out of your hand."

He says to me, "Wait a minute, what is you doing?"

I said, "Imma straighten up the cards? I'm finna deal us a new hand."

He said, "Nah you not."

I'm like, "What you mean man, 'nah I'm not, I just cooned on you?"

He said, "Nah you ain't wait a minute." Then he threw down another ace, then another ace, then he threw down a third ace — which made four aces...

Mockingly, he said, "I wasn't disbanding, I was just spreading slow. Do you see what I'm trying to show you? Sometimes people have a tendency to lay their hand down slow. And you make your move too soon, to know what's on your mind. Nah, you clowning me and carrying on and you done lost. You didn't even know you lost because, as I said, I disband slow."

I never forgot that, then he got up and clowned me. So that's a good lesson in life, that I got out of Sonny. You gotta wait before you start celebrating on somebody else's mistake 'cause you never know. That mistake just might be disbanding slow...

So after we played a while, he said man, I wish we had some money, so we can get us some blow or go out to party, and I looked at him real good. I said, "Sonny boy, you know what? We been in this hotel for two or three days now, man. You think it's about time for us to get out and do something?"

He said, "Yeah man, but shit, people ain't brought the money by me. We ain't got no money, what we gon do?"

I said, "Wait a minute, Sonny Boy, look at this." I went down in my sock and I pulled out a big bankroll. It was about twenty-five hundred dollars or so. I threw it up in the air, and money came down like confetti.

And he said, "Ohh! Geney Boy, where you get that from?"

I said, "Sonny this is your money the whole time I was just holding it. Because you was throwing it away so fast. So you can have money later on like now man."

Boy he grabbed me and he just pinched my head. Wrestled me on the floor, we went out in the street. He said, "You my boy! You my boy, Geney Boy! You love me, don't you?"

I said, "Yeah, Sonny Boy, I know you messed up and throw away too much money man. And I had to slow you down."

He say, "Yeah well you slowed me down enough, let's call Manzel." Boy he was so happy, he was so happy. The one thing he was happy about is that, that's what he really in his heart knew that he could trust me with anything and everything, because I could have gotten away with that money. He would have never known it, there was nowhere in my mind or heart... I had no thoughts about doing him dirty like that, or anybody else. I was just trying to just save him from himself, and to let him have that money at a better time. And that was no better time than right then.

Then I looked him in the face and said, "Guess what Sonny?"

He said, "What?"

I say, "I just disband slow." Boy he died laughing, he loved that he died laughing. Sonny was funny man.

Eventually, we came to the hotel. Manzel was at the hotel and he didn't have nothing with em. He done sold at that 'cause he was doing big business at that time. He said, "Hey Sonny, some people want to meet you and Geney Boy up in Beverly Hills." It was a house full of pimps, they were having a big party in a mansion. This guy was named Hippie, he sent Manzel down in his Rolls-Royce to come pick us up.

We got into the car, I said, "Man Sonny, what kind of car is this?"

He said, " It's a Rolls-Royce."

I said, "Aw man, this ain't no Rolls-Royce." I never believed it was a Rolls-Royce because it was so new I had never seen that body style before. We pulled over to Seven-Eleven to get some papers to roll some weed. I went around the front and there it was — *"RR"*. I said, Man, if the boys back home could see me now, nobody would believe that I was riding in a Rolls-Royce.

We drove through Hollywood and made it to Beverly Hills. Before you knew it we was up on Coldwater Canyon. We rode through the hills and there it was a big huge mansion, with the gates and the long driveway, the big lights in front of the house, pulled and walked up. Manzel rang the doorbell — a long chime rang.

The big huge doors opened and there she was. A great big fine redhead stallion. Stared us in the face and she saw Sonny and just almost melted. She was just like a groupie when she seen Sonny. Because he was just such a legendary person, that some people were just impressed that they would be just totally mesmerized. She could hardly get her breath, she announced, "Sonny's here! Sonny's here! Sonny's here!" Everybody started coming towards the foyer to meet us.

It was a huge mansion sorta like the Playboy Mansion, I'd never seen nothing like that before. I looked around and all the guys was dressed like I was dressed. They has the blue sleeves and the bell bottoms, the long collar and hats drop down. I never seen anything like it, at this magnitude. I've seen some pimps have a Cadillac, a little apartment or small house. But this was like the superfly era, a mansion with a big foyer, huge chandelier and hallway, with winding staircases. Boy, they was walking around there with jewels, diamonds, and stuff. The hoes was laying around, I mean this was Hollywood motion picture looking stuff.

And I'm saying to myself, Man! Look at this action! I'm knowing I'm going to be like this sooner or later. Imma get into all this action because I know I'm just as good as these cats up here. Because I knew some cold-blooded gangsters back home, but they weren't open to the opportunity that these guys out here on the West Coast were. And I knew that I had them under control as far as my presence as a player. Man, shit, I knew I was 'gon get a chot like this here.

The broads was just winkin' and blinkin' at us because they knew that Sonny was a big check, that Sonny would buy and spend money on sex and drugs like a ramped fool. Everybody could make money on Sonny, they really brought Sonny over there to bait 'em in. To try and break 'em but they didn't know that they had me to deal with, or where I was comin' from because I was a little youngster. As far as they were concerned, I was just a young naive kid who didn't know no better. I'm just hanging out with Sonny and they can play the game anyway. But I was way up on their thing, I knew exactly where they were coming from. So I knew I had Sonny's back all the way it went.

And a few minutes later, Hippie came down the steps. He looked just like a statue, man. He looked like a Greek God — he had a gold outfit on – it looked like fourteen karat gold – chains around his neck, two girls on his arm, and a long hair perm. He comes down the steps looking like Billy D. Williams didn't have nothing on him. He walks in, real tall dude, very impressive. When he walked in the room all the fellas that was there, his partner's more or less. They was just bowing down like he was a Mexican general. Oh man, it was Hippie baby this and Hippie baby that. Sonny was just looking at like 'Okay, what you want? I'm here'.

He gets to Sonny grabs him by the shoulders and hugs him, as if to make the impression that Sonny and him were old partners, and been down with each other the whole time. I knew better than this, Sonny was looking like who in the fuck you think you is to touch me? He was being cool about it, he knew that it was a reason why he pulled him there. Because basically Sonny would have gone off. He was just as crazy, just as drunk as he could be. Had been drinking on that Smirnoff Vodka and we have been smoking that weed all the way to the house. So Sonny introduced me to Hippie and we shook hands, we did a lil' slick talk.

He asked Sonny, he say, "Hey man what you want, champagne, blow, a girl? Whatever you want man, the party is on me."

Sonny said, "Well hey, bring it on."

He went in his little stash, and he opened a pill box. He used his gold spoon from around his neck and shoveled about six to eight hits, a gram or so. He put it on an album, and Sonny hit it. He said to me, I hit it. A couple other guys hit it, and then somebody said well let's divi up, let's really get some of this thang! So, Sonny looks at me and winks his eyes, because Sonny knew that it was a setup.

He said, "Well I'll put in fifty dollars."

Everyone looks around and says fifty dollars? They knew about Sonny, and heard about him putting up five hundred, two hundred, some real money, but he said fifty dollars this time. One guy said, "Cool, well, I'll put up fifty." Another guy put up fifty and one guy put up one hundred, Hippie put up a couple hundred. So now they got a nice little thang, Manzel breaks it off and gives them about a half an ounce. First time they put in they put down a sixteenth almost, eight ball. Everyone took a little hit and passed it to Sonny, Sonny winked his eye and passed it to me.

He whispered, "Geney Boy, get all you want." I hit it and took the card two or three times. I could not do that much 'cause I was still a rookie. Sonny took out a hundred-dollar bill and rolled it up. He lined it up, and he took with one nostril he took damn near almost half of it. Then he took another big hit with the other side and said, "Ahhh!", popped his fingers and just about all of it was gone.

One of the dudes said, "Man what the fuck he done tooted it all."

Sonny said, " Well shit, I paid my money for it."

The dude said, "I don't give a fuck what you paid for, you done tooted it all man, that ain't right."

So Sonny started to talk real loud. Hippie said, "Well it ain't no thing we got some more."

Sonny did the same thing when it came back around to him again. Now it was about to be a hoopla in that place, Hippie tried to cool it down. He cooled it down, he gave the boys some more for themselves. He took us to another room, he took us to another room where there were a bunch of girls in the room. Sonny saw one that he liked, and man, the first thing Hippie did was give the girl a hundred-dollar bill from his big bankroll. He told her to take care of Sonny right away. It was all Sonny needed, man, Sonny went back there and bumped this girl off — dogged her out so bad she's just screaming hollering, he was up there laughing like hell. We both knew that Sonny was hung like a horse, and he was probably trying to take it all out on her. Plus he was full of that vodka and full of that cocaine. So she was having a problem, and everybody was waiting to see how she looked when she came out. When she came out her wig was all crooked and everything.

Sonny was so happy he didn't know what to do, and he said, "Well, hey, what you 'gon do about Geney Boy? Geney Boy needs a girl, too."

Hippie looks at me and he says, "Pick which one you want."

Sonny says, "No, I want him to fuck that same bitch I had 'cause that bitch pussy, big hole bitch is good. Geney Boy, you got to fuck this bitch. She can suck a dick, boy." You know he always wanted me to have the best of what he had. He always wanted that.

Normally I would fuck 'em first. But I said. "Ok, I'm 'gon fuck the same bitch that Sonny wanted me to fuck."

I took her back to the room; she gave me some head. This bitch deep throat, she just swallowed my little dick. Oh man, I mean toes spread, she hit me hard man. I fucked her man, I fucked her good, I fucked her everywhere except under the arm and in the eye. I was a young boy and I was having a ball, I thought.

So eventually we went back to tootin' cocaine. I got back and Sonny started to laugh, he said. "What did you think of her, Geney Boy?"

I said, "That big hole bitch sho' got a good mouth I damn near fell over."

And he just died laughing. Hippie said, "Y'all ok?"

I say, "We got to go home man, cause we got an early appointment to see Sammy and some other stuff to do tomorrow."

So Hippie took us home, we got on got in the back of the Rolls-Royce and we rode off from the mansion. But down on Worshire, and when we got out, Hippie gave Sonny a package. They talked a little bit and we went on about our business, exchange numbers and stuff. That was the last time I seen him, Manzel and the rest of those guys. But it was a big occasion. It was some game that I was really thirsty to see in real time. There I was in the middle of it, I got a chance to see that there is some bigger game going on. That I could fit into and be a part of, I could be a dominant force if I stayed out there.

So we finally made it back to the hotel and chit-chatted for a minute. Went on up to the suite and hung out a little bit. We had like a nice little piece of blow then we finished it. Soon I started to come down, and face reality that we eventually got to see Sammy Davis. Because Sammy had been gone all the while we was in Los Angeles. At least they left us a message that Sammy was not available, that he would be there next week. They left that message because I'm sure the doorman told Sammy that we came and how drunk Sonny was, what it looked like, and he had already had a bad conversation with Sammy's wife before we left there.

When we was talking about coming, Sammy might have been ducking us.

I can't swear by that, so we never did get a chance to see him. He was always elusive as far as I was concerned, 'cause I could see this. I figured the best thing we could do is get one more chance to see Sammy because I was desperate. I wanted to see him and meet him so bad. Sonny was building me up, to how Sammy would be able to help us. Sonny was hoping that what I was thinking wasn't true and that his credibility was gone. Because he was holding up by telling me that he could see Sammy whenever he wanted. So, I was going to give him all the benefit of the doubt, we just sat up in the room for a day or so, hoping that Sammy would get in touch with us.

But in the meantime, we began to look at each other kinda strange, we said hey man don't you feel kinda funny? We both agreed. Come to find out that the broad that me and him bumped off over at the Hippie's house done had the claps, he had done caught 'em, I had done caught 'em. She had 'em and we was dripping like a running faucet right away. Boy he was so mad he didn't know what to do. I was upset about it, but we both had to laugh, we brought it on our own self. So he calls the Black lady and she comes over and he tells her what the situation is.

He wants a doctor to come to the room and take care of both of us. Because he doesn't want to go back to Las Vegas, Geraldine to his wife, it takes about three days to get rid of it, so we go to sit it out in Los Angeles at the hotel until we get better and the doctor comes over. So then he tells the doctor to give him some pills.

The doctor say, "I don't have any pills. I got this double-stranded penicillin, I'll give him a shot. A couple days y'all should be straight and be alright."

Sonny said, "No. I'm not gonna take no shot." Sonny, I found out was cold-blood scared shitless of needles. He hated the thought of needles, just like some people are scared of rattlesnakes. He was scared of needles, that's one reason in the overall end of it all. I knew that Sonny could have never shot himself and killed himself in the end — because he was scared of death needles and I had to damn near kiss his ass to let the doctor shoot him up with that little needle of penicillin to get rid of those claps.

I begged him. "Sonny Boy, please let them man shoot you, you big ol' dude you can take it."

And Sonny was about to cry. He said, "I don't want no shot, I don't want it."

I said, "Please man, please Sonny Boy, we can't go back unless you let the man shoot you to get rid of these claps. We can't even go back to get those hoes in Hookernook." I tried everything that I could think of to let him give this man the opportunity to shoot him with the penicillin.

So Sonny said, "Ok man, I'll do it."

I said, "Well turn your head Sonny." He turned his head like a little girl.

The man said, "Bang! Bang!" and it was over with.

We said, " See, that didn't hurt."

He said, "Nah, that didn't hurt." And we bust out laughing.

That's why I know Sonny Boy really ain't no needle man.

Sonny's Shadow

So we've sat it out in a hotel for a few days, until we finally got rid of the claps, and headed back to Las Vegas. We was laughing every now and then; we bust out laughing about the issue. That happen ovah at the hippie's house, and we started to thinkin' about those girls.

I said, "We gone have to be careful man, n' foolin' with them wayward ass hoes."

He bust out laughing and say, "What, you talkin' about them big hole bitches?"

I say, "Yeah man, cause' sometimes you can fall in and can't come out."

He say, "Yeah! Like we just did."

So we ridin' down the highway and he asked me a question. He had asked this question before, but he asked it again. He said, "Gene?" He said, "Geney boy, if we was in the desert going across the Baja, and we only had just one lil' bottle of water, would you drink it or would you give it to me?"

I said, "Sonny boy, you know I told you before I'd give it to you."

He said, "Why?"

I said, "Because... you strong enough to carry me across the desert, but I'm too little to carry you across the desert. So if you can survive, I'll survive. That means that we will survive."

He looked at me n' tears come in his eyes, and he say, "You my boy, Geney boy." So we just rolled on down the highway. We was quiet for a minute, then something came to me, to ask him some questions.

I said, "Sonny..." I said, "Let me ask you a question that I wanted to ask you all the time. Could you have beaten Muhammad Ali?"

He said, "Geney boy, I threw one fight and I lost the other fight." He said, "...and boy, he fights like a girl. He hit and he run: and he run and he hits. He ain't gon stand there and fight 'like a man, but ain't nobody gon' ever beat him no more." He say, "I was the only chance that they had at beatin' him, they ain't gon ever beat him no mo'"

And I let it rest at that. He kept on talkin' about the final punch money, he said, "Geney boy..." He say, "I'm gon' have this money soon, imma take care of you. I know you've done been away from your family awhile and I'm gonna make sure that you have enough to take care of them. Because I've got enough comin' from this final punch money."

I say, "Well I sho' could use it, cause' my ol' lady is on my ass about comin' home. And my momma's on my ass about comin' home, and the baby's gettin' older and older; and I don't know what to do. I can't stay out here no longer — I gotta go home sooner or later."

He said, "Geney boy, say, well maybe we can figure somethin' — you can bring your family out here. And just hang out with me after."

I said, "Sonny, no, I don't really want to bring my family out here. I wanna just leave it like it is, and hopefully something big can happen, that I can take care of them from here."

So we rode on back and we went on back to Las Vegas. And we sat around, we didn't do nothing. I sat around the hotel and gambled a little bit. He'd sit there and he went home. Geraldine was always bitchin', like he knew she was gon' be doin'. And he'd play with Donnelle, who was the love of his life, and so one day he came over to my house, and he said, "Geney boy..." He say, "I got ah... I wanna go to Reno and let's party a lil' bit, 'cause I got a fight comin' up. And I wanna party just one mo' time before we go to the fight."

I said, "Ok, yeah."

He say, "Go get Tony!"

Tony was the White boy that played – 'fake played' – with us in the band. Sonny liked em, I liked him, so I said, "Yeah, let's go get Tony."

So we went and got Tony, and we rolled up to Reno, Nevada. We got to Reno and it was late that evening, and it was a lil' bitty Las Vegas. But

I kinda liked it, they had whorehouse's up there, up a storm! Back in those days...

And Sonny used to wanna stop in because he knew the owners of the whorehouses. And we stopped in and hollered at a few people that he knew, and told them, well, we'll be back. And we gon' party before we go out, 'cause he got a fight comin' up and he's gonna try to just party a lil' bit before the fight.

Right now he's gotta to go to training, so we went into the Harris Club, the Harris Club brothers... When we walked in there, everybody was lookin' at us. But he had started drinkin' again, he started to gettin' fucked up. And everybody was lookin' at us, talking about that's Sonny Liston, that's Sonny Liston. And then one guy ol' cowboy lookin' guy with a cowboy hat on – he looked like Texas Riddle or somebody – he was a big ol' tall guy; he was about as big as Sonny.

He say, "Hey! Boy, come here."

Sonny looked at him strange like, whatcha mean 'hey boy come here?' He say, "Don't I know you?"

Sonny looked at him and say, "Yeah, I'm Willie Mays... Willie Mays, the ball player."

He say, "Yeah?"

He says, "Come ovah here and play a lil' poker with me."

Sonny said, "Ok, fine." So Sonny walked over there, and sat down at the table.

The guy gave Sonny about two or three hundred-dollar chips — black chips. Sonny cashed them in and made, gottem a good twenty-dollar chips and then started to play poker. So, Sonny was winnin' a lil' bit and the guy was winnin' a lil' bit. So they was doing pretty good and they was having a good time. All of a sudden, Sonny pulled out a four of a kind and won a big pot, and he bust out laughin' and he jumped up out the seat. And he bust out laughin', 'cause he's been sneaking me chips behind his back all this time for us to save, to make sure we had some more extra money.

When he got ready to sit back down, there was an old White woman — another blue-eyed White woman. She was kinda like uh... a lady Ku Klux Klan. And as soon as Sonny got ready to sit back down, she scooted him up under his seat. And scooted up under em, and Sonny accidentally sat in her lap a little bit, and jumped up and said, "Woah!"

And she say, "Didn't you see me sittin' in this seat?"

He said, "Miss, I was already in the seat."

She replied, "You damn, dumb-ass nigger, you sittin' down there on top of me!"

Sonny said, "Lady, you don't have to talk to me like that."

The dude said — the guy that had gave em the chips – initially, said, "Hey man, you ain't gon be able to talk to a woman like this. Get the fuck up from this table!" He said that to Sonny, and Sonny looked at him strange. 'Cause sometimes Sonny didn't get any subject matter that people would bring him.

And the first thing that I said was, "Sonny! You gon let that son of a bitch talk to us like that? Us like that?"

Sonny turned around and said, "Hell no!" and grabbed 'em and smacked 'em in the face. He turned the poker table over, the woman got to screamin' "Ahh! Ahh!" Sonny got to kickin' him in his ass, and he turned the poker table over. The poker chips went everywhere, now he done turned the casino out. Everybody said 'Lord, have mercy, Sonny Liston done went crazy in here'. So, we just got our little money and went on the elevator, and went up to our floor.

A little later on the security guard knocks on the door, boom! Boom! Boom! Boom! Boom!

"Sonny boy, let us in here, Sonny boy, let us in here."

He opened the door he say, "Gene open the balcony door, imma start throwin' these mother fuckers up outta here as soon as they come in the door." I did what he said, I opened up the balcony, and I opened up the front door. And he started to tusslin' wit 'me – about twelve of 'me – grabbed them down and ruffin' them up. I'm in the middle of it, we all husslin' and shit. Tony's in the middle of it; we all husslin' and shit.

Before you know it, Sonny said, "Ok ya'll, we'll get the fuck up outta this raggedy ass joint."

They escorted us through the casino, everybody lookin' talking about that's Sonny Liston, that's Sonny Liston. They put us in our car and drove us down the hill with a police escort — about four or five motorcycles to get us down the hill in Reno, for us to be able to get out of their town. That was so funny; we didn't know nothing but to laugh our ass off. We still had the chips — we never could cash them in, but we still had the chips. We headed down the hill, headed back to Las Vegas.

So, as soon as we got back to Las Vegas, Sonny went home to recuperate. I went back to the hotel; Tony went back to his apartment. A couple days passed by, Sonny started to sweatin' it out, he called me over. We went to the Riviera Gym, up on the top floor of the Riviera, where all of the fighters used to train at and they still did up until they tore it down.

But anyway, Sonny started to let me train him. I couldn't do nothing with the medicine ball. The medicine ball was just too big and heavy, I couldn't throw it. He'd throw the medicine ball at his own self. So, all of a sudden, there was a wrestler. A big heavyweight wrestler who was also working out and training in the gym. And he made some comment about me throwin' the medicine ball at Sonny. Like I threw it like a lil' sissy or somethin', and Sonny heard em. And Sonny told 'em say, "I'll kick you off in yo ass. You wrestlin' son of a bitch, you talkin' to Geney boy. Don't you ever say somethin' to Geney boy like he's a bitch or somethin'."

I say, "It's ok."

Sonny say, "No, it ain't ok." He said, "Matter a fact, get yo punk ass on up outta here."

The dude he was bigger than Sonny, but he was just a bunch of steroids. Sonny was all man. He got his ass up outta there with the quickness, and Sonny say, "I told you he wasn't nothing but a big ol' punk." So we just kept right on working out.

Then all sudden I got an emergency call from my mom sayin' that I got to come home. 'Cause my ol' lady she's runnin' around kinda loose, and I need to be there to take care of her and my baby. So, I say, "Well, I'll- I'll do what I can to get home as soon as I can get there."

I talked to Sonny and I said Sonny, "I need some money, man. I need some money man to get back home."

He say, "Geney boy, you don't have to go, man, I'll send em some money down there to take care of em."

I said, "Nah, Sonny, I've got to go back home, man, things is going crazy in my house."

So he called my mom, which he used to call her 'moms' every time he talked to her. He said. "Moms, I'll take care of Geney boy."

She say, "Nah, send em home, he needs to go home, he needs to come home."

So he say, "Well, I'll send him home next week."

He moped around, he was just real sad because he didn't want to see me leave. He said, "Man, you know we bout' to get back on top again, I got the fight comin' down here: I'll be able to have some money and break you off and we can get started, and we can do these TV shows and all the other stuff that we got lined up — we gon' do Ed Sullivan Show, we gon' go back to Mr. Paige and get some movies and everything."

He said, "Don't leave, Geney boy."

I said. " Sonny, I've got to leave, man... " I say, "My family's at stake now, I can't just hang around no more."

So he said, "I'll call you next week, and I take to the airport and I'll buy you a ticket to go home."

Alright, we pass by he came and got me at the apartment and said 'pack ya stuff.' "I'm finna let you go home."

Then on the way to the highway down at the McCrary Airport he started to cryin' in the car. He said, "Geney boy ain't I been good by you? Why you want to leave man, you know you're the only friend I got here!"

I said to Sonny, "I got to man 'cause my wife and my family n' everybody is on my ass. I done been here over a year and I got to go back home."

He said, "Man, but I've been good by you, Geney boy, say don't leave me man... I hate to see you go 'cause you the only somebody that I can trust."

I said, "Sonny, I'll be back, just let me go home and check on my folks and see what is happenin'."

He said, "Imma call you. When I say the worst, the worst is worser than the worst. Please come 'cause it's gonna be bad. There's some thangs that's going on that I can't tell you about. It's going to be rough for us, for a minute. And I know that you can keep it straight, because you a straight shooter, you always get it straight for me."

So we finally made it to McCarran Airport, he walked to the gate with me. Right then, they used to have where you could just look right through the gate and see people boarding the plane. And he was standing up besides the gate, just looking through the gate, with tears rollin' down his eyes. He was wavin' at me like this goin' to be the last time that Imma ever see you, I betcha.

Ironically, it was... I got up on the plane and I flew off, I was all teary-eyed really hurting cause' I didn't wanna leave my friend like that. I knew he needed me and I knew that I was keepin' him alive. Because we had a lot of experiences that now I understand, why he was so skeptical about so many people around him that he didn't know. And he would just watch cars behind us and make quick turns and stuff like that. I could never understand back in the day what was causing him to be that panicky; but in the end it came to me.

Bad News

I finally got back home to St. Louis, they had almost gave me a ticket tape parade. Everybody was so happy that I came back, that I was victorious, that I had been with Sonny Liston. Cause' they was gettin' blow-by-blow reports on the radio about my adventures out there in Las Vegas with Sonny Liston. And my cousin Marvin Louis was tellin' everything that was goin' on. So they was listening to him and he would put a lil' sugar coat on it, before you know it, I was the talk of the town. Richard and 'em was workin' in a lil' rinky-dinky club, they came and begged me to get back with 'em.

For a while, I got back with 'em and sang a lil' bit, but my heart wasn't there. It was kinda rough after I'd seen the big time and knew what the big time was about. Them lil' stinky clubs that we had been singin' in I used to think was so big and so good wasn't nothing no more.

I called Sonny, he say, "Geney boy, I'm glad to hear from you, I'm goin' down to Texas and have a fight. But I gotta get out the hospital first."

I said, "Whatcha mean you gotta get out the hospital?"

He said man, "When I dropped you off at the airport, an eighteen-wheeler truck ran over my car and it almost killed me."

"An eighteen-wheeler truck?" I said. Not knowin' that was a hit squad tryin' to hit him I believe to this day, the reason why the truck ran over him. He had glass and stuff all in his face. Sonny stayed in the hospital so long that they kept him under observation. They treated him with intravenous penicillin to try to keep his fever and stuff down, 'cause of the accident.

He had called Scrap Iron Johnson to spar with 'em, but Scrap Iron couldn't spar with 'me, because he was in no condition. But he still was trying to take the fight, 'cause he needed the money. I didn't know that he was in as bad as the shape that he was in. So I used to take his phone calls, he would call down to Johnny Dawn's beauty parlor, that's where I always used to hang out. All the fellas would talk to Sonny on the phone, he would be so glad to talk to the homeboys, 'cause he felt like he was getting closer to me when he was talkin' to my friends and stuff. He would be so excited, he would always ask me, "Geney boy, when are you coming back?"

I'd say, "I'd be right back after Christmas."

He'd say, "I'll tell you what, Geraldine is comin' to St. Louis to be with her family for Christmas. When she comes to St. Louis, you jump on the plane. I'll send you a ticket, and you come back out here. We'll go down to Mexico and we'll party a lil' bit after the fight."

I said, "Ok, cool." But I knew my momma was gonna raise hell at the thought that I was gon be headed back to Las Vegas to spend the Christmas with Sonny, and knowing that my family needed me. The baby was gettin' older as I said, and my wife she was gettin' disappointed with me goin' down there with Sonny; she just didn't know what to think. My sister had a baby while I was gone and the house was just too tight. They needed me there to try to make something happen for the family.

But I knew my chances would have been better if I would have stayed out there with Sonny. 'Cause the opportunities was better; there wasn't not opportunities in St. Louis. So as time went by, it started gettin' closer and closer to Christmas. I was waiting to hear from Sonny every day, and he said, "Man, I'm gonna send you the money to get back out here for Christmas." So, it got closer to the time, the next thing I knew, no one was answering the phone. I called every day — no one was answerin' the phone. I called him two or three times a day. No one was answerin' the phone.

And then it was Christmas... Then it was the day after Christmas. No one was answerin' the phone and I was wondering what was happening to Sonny.

Somewhere along the line, the news hit that Sonny Liston was dead. He had been killed in his home by being struck over the neck with a table — and overdosed on a heroin coke hotshot. And I knew better than that 'cause I knew Sonny wasn't gonna hotshot himself, 'cause he didn't shoot no dope. Because I couldn't hardly make him take the penicillin shot for the claps.

It was just- it was a horrible story, I couldn't believe it. People was callin' me from all over the country, 'cause everybody knew that I was out there with Sonny and wanted to know what happened. Geraldine had gotten back home, found him on the floor dead.

It was such a hard break. I cried for at least a week, then I went down and begged my momma to give me some plane fare. I went back down to Sonny's funeral, I stayed with Geraldine in their house. That's when I got a chance to meet his children and a bunch more other people who was friends with Sonny. And Geraldine was very nice to me, I must say. She let me drive his cars, I went over to the West Side and everybody was real sad for me because they thought I was Sonny's son.

And then I went over on the strip. The police stopped me on the strip in Sonny's car and told me if I don't get my Black ass over there on the West Side, where I belong, that they was gonna lock me up, and kick my ass, because I had to have at least a work permit to be over on the strip. Back in those days, the Las Vegas strip was a straight apartheid, all I can think of was that if Sonny was with me, they would have never did me like, and I just began to miss him more and more.

The funeral day came, we all rolled over in the limousines to the funeral parlor. It was jam-packed with nothin' but stars, so I sat down in a seat right beside Ed Sullivan and Sergio Funky. We sat there, Ed Suvillian was trying to pet me up because I was just tore apart at Sonny being dead like that. Aand everybody know there was some hanky-panky involved, but everybody was trying to be quiet about it, nobody was really mentioning it, and I couldn't understand that. Then the Inkspots got up and sung that song, '*Sonny thank you for the sunshine in your smile...*' They did that song, they did a slow version, and in the middle of the song, Eddie Turf, the old mustache Harry, jumped up and said, "Sonny Boy! Sonny Boy! They shouldn't have done you like that! You didn't mean nobody no harm, why did they do you like that?"

I could never understand, they had to take him out of the church, he was so emotional about Sonny being dead. Eddie Turf really did love Sonny, even though he was a gangster; but he did love Sonny. And Ed Suvillian and 'em was tryin' to pet me up, tellin' me it was going to be alright.

I looked back at the back of the church as we were about to go out, and there she was, Connie Shaw, the lil' White girl that had dogged out and took to California, that ran off with the toga sheet on. She ran up to me and she grabbed me, she held me tight and said, "I'm so sorry about your friend Sonny Liston, I cried myself to the thought that something bad happened to him. 'Cause even though we had our days and ups and downs, we did have some fun; and I do love him."

That was the most gratifying thing I ever heard coming from someone that should have hated us, by the way we treated this girl. Today I would have never did that, but I guess that's just the way of life, being in the game. So, we all went into the cars, limousines, and followed the hearse headed down to the strip. All the dealers and every casino was out on the curb, with their hand over their heart, as to recognize Sonny as one of them, that they really did love, even though he did cause havoc and had the most roudy-roughest of times that you could ever have. They still loved him, and Sonny was still their boy.

We finally got to the cemetery, and we took the casket out the hearse, and Joe Lewis carried the casket, I carried the casket, Sergio Funky and 'em carried the casket, the gangsters carried the casket. Joe Lewis made a comment and said, "Sonny may have drawn more people at the funeral than he did at the fight." Everybody bust on laughin' but Sonny loved Joe Louis and Joe Lewis loved Sonny.

Because I remember Sonny took me once to see Joe Louis at Caesars Palace. I wanted to meet Joe Louis so bad because I had heard so much about him as a kid, being our hero as a prize fighter, and Sonny took me down there just to meet Joe Louis — I never will forget it. There was a lot of champions down in the basement hanging out in Caesars Palace. At the sports bars where Joe Louis was the greeter down there, they all wanted to hang out and be around Joe Louis. I'll never forget it, I asked Sonny – he was a great big ol' guy – I said, "Sonny, I know you don't want to fight this guy."

Sonny said, "Shit! I'd knock him out in six." He said, "See that guy over there?" Another big ol' guy. "I'd knock him out in eight!" He said, "See that guy over there? He broke and ran from six rounds until I knocked him out in the back of the head!" Sonny was a character man, and Joe Louis loved him. I asked Joe would he take a picture with me and he said he would. But I could never get around to get the picture took with me and Sonny and him — that would have been a classic picture today. Gene "Poo Poo Man" Anderson of the Parliament Funkadelic PFunk Allstars, who I became. Sonny Liston and Joe "Bomber" Louis down there in Caesars Palace in those days. That would have been an iconic picture and I hate that I didn't take the picture, because I was tryin' to find a cameraman. But I got kinda like starstruck and didn't do it, and I hate myself once again, for not taking that iconic picture.

But anyway, Joe Louis sat there, and he lowered the casket – him and some more mob guys – lowered the casket into the ground, and we did the ashes to ashes and the dust to dust. I'm crying like a lil' bitch, and so we finally left, and we went back to the International Hilton Hotel.

That's where they had the meet and greet, over there all the people that was friendly towards Sonny. I guess you could call it a pass ova', I guess that's what they call it. Anyway, I was all discombobulated, I was all torn up and everybody that knew me, knew Sonny. They was comin' up to me talkin' bout how sad they was about Sonny bein' demised like he had been. They knew that me and Sonny was tight. Everybody in the whole town knew that Sonny was reborn again when I came into his life.

I saw a guy by the name of Ernest Shore. He was a comedian, he said 'Oh yeah!' He saw me and called me over to him, and he petted me up. And I had some copies of our records, the Sonny Liston record. I gave him a copy of the record and I told 'em what was happenin'.

Then I saw my man Redd Foxx, at the Hilton Hotel, we was all there in the lobby. And he called me ova' to 'em and he say, "Son I'm- I'm sorry about what happened for you…"

But I said, "here's a copy of the record that we recorded. It's a shame that my career's all gon cause' Sonny's gone."

Redd said, "Man listen, Imma give you some good advice, if somethin' going on that you don't know what's goin' on, and you outta know what's goin' on. Or there's somethin' goin' on, that you don't know that's goin' on, and everybody think you know what's goin' on. Or there's somethin' that you need to know, that you don't know, that you should know. Either way, it's too big for you. You need to go home to St. Louis and get away from here, because it's more to it than meets the eye about Sonny."

I said. "Yeah Redd, but what am I gon' do about my career? I ain't got no where to go, no place to do nothin' wit. It's all over when Sonny died."

He said, "Well listen, I got somethin' for you…" He reached in his pocket and he pulled out a card. And he say, "As long as this guy is alive, you got somebody that's on your side." And I took the card and I turned the card over. It was a picture of him.

I said, "Redd this is a picture of you!"

He said, "Well, ain't I somebody? As long as I'm livin' you'll always have some place, and someone to depend on and somebody to help you with your life and career. As long as I'm livin'." He gave me a hundred-dollar bill, and he say, "You go back home to St. Louis, and I'll come get you one day."

Every Day is Christmas

A So I went back home to St. Louis and I stay about twelve years or so. I did a lot of things between that time, I got record contracts. I did a lot of exposure because I had been with Sonny, and not only that I got to be kinda famous on my own. And I learned how to do things on my own, without the assistance or dependin' upon Sonny or anybody. I made it to the top and I rode on, until one day about ten or twelve years later, after Redd had made it.

He had made it to be the number one comedy variety show in America — *Sanford and Son*. And he left the show, and he had a show in Las Vegas. He came home to St. Louis, they named a street after him called the Redd Foxx Lane. Him and Night Train Lane and Prince Spencer, the tap dancer for *Four Stepbrothers*. Redd came down for the crowning of his block that he grew up in St. Louis and he saw me. He was so glad to see me. He say, "Whatcha been doin'?"

I told 'em, all the things I'd been doin'. He did a show at the Paul Symphony Hall. He had me with 'em all together, all the way, him and my cousin Marvin Louis. I was with 'em all the way and he finally left, and he say come on back to Las Vegas if you ready right now. So shortly after that, I got a group of guys together from back home, and we went on back out to Las Vegas.

He was a big star, he had done made it to where he wanted to go. He had a big huge show comin' up at the Hacienda Hotel. So I was at a dinky-ass hotel called the Blue Angel, and a club called the Blue Angel. And I was singin' over there and he was raisin' so much hell, me and the group called *Paperbag* from St. Louis. We was raisin' so much hell people was comin' from near and far to see our show. Then one day a guy named Bay Boo, was Sonny's friend who owns a hotel called "Towne Tavern," had heard about us. Heard that I was back in town, Sonny's lil' partner, and he came ova' there to see out act. When he came over to see our act the fellas was like stuck up against me. Always was some shit when it came down to me, I guess I was so good and so young them days, that I was a terrible to em, so they was just selfish. And he came ova' there, Bay Boo, and a guy named QB. And Bay Boo said, "Where's the lil' guy wit the long perm?"

They said, "You talkin' about Gene Anderson, 'Poo Poo Man'."

He say, "Yeah."

They said he's in the bedroom sleepin'.

"Go get em'."

And he said to me, "Listen, I wanna see your act wit these guys."

So I did my lil' act and he told the guys — he made it just straight-forward. "This guy has been out here before wit Sonny, and he proved to be one of the best. We wanna give y'all a shot at our club, but if you don't bring him, no shot."

"Oh yeah, they'll bring me, they'll bring me..."

So, we got a lil' job at the Plaza, down there at the Las Vegas club. And then we finally went ova' there to the uh the Town Tavern. The place was closed down for I don't know how long, all of a sudden we started to play in there. They took us ova' there they gave us a hundred dollars apiece a night. And they gave us food – that's what we started out with – and before you knew it, people was screamin' to get into the place. It was overloaded, packed with different stars and stuff. They had come to see our show. We had kicked out a big show ova' there.

And they took a picture of me and blew the picture up bigger than life-size and put it on the wall besides Billie Holiday and Kyle Bassie and the rest of 'em. And the fellas went crazy behind it, they couldn't believe that they would do that, and didn't do them. But what they didn't know was that I already had a reputation from bein' wit Sonny Liston.

And I done came back, I ran into a dude named Jones who was Sonny's trainer. He was called Sergeant Jones — he was in the army. He had gotten out and he was Redd Foxx's head of security. He said, "Hey, is this you, Gene?"

I said, "Yeah!"

He was so glad to see me he just grabbed me and hugged me. He said, "Does Redd know you're in town?"

I said, "Nah, man."

I told him the ol' story of what did happen' with the band and all that kinda shit – the crybaby shit – and he said, "Listen, Redd will be in town today, I'm goin' to the airport to pick him up. Would you like to go with me to go and find Redd?"

I said, "Yeah ok, that's cool to pick him up."

So we drove there to McCarran Airport, and Redd was gettin' off. He was in his red Mercedes. And we was in the *Sanford & Son* red truck, and we spotted them comin' down the highway. He saw me, he almost wrecked the car, he was blowin' the horn and stuff, and we was wavin' at each other racin' down the highway. He speed up, we speed up, he speed up, we speed up. Then we finally got to the house, he grabbed me, hugged me and kissed me and started cryin'. 'Cause Redd was very sentimental that I had made it back — Sonny's boy had made it back.

And he took me in the house and the first thing he did was take his switchblade knife out. He thrown it and stuck it in the wall, told me to go get it. Then told me to stick it in the wall. I stuck it in the wall. Then he and I proceeded to do it again and again, we chopped the wall up laughin' like hell. He had a Christmas tree up, I say. "Redd, whatcha doin' wit a Christmas tree up this time?"

He said, "Christmas is every day I'm alive."

A strange feeling came over me. Redd was there and was now a big superstar and Sonny was gone. I felt as if half of my life got gone with Sonny. And so I didn't know what to do.

I didn't know how to approach Redd. But I asked him reluctantly, "Hey Redd, could you give me a shot on your show? The one that's coming up at the Hacienda?"

He said, "Yeah, Jones, I'll tell you what I want you to do. I want you to go down there tonight, bring Geney Boy with you, and tell Prince to put him on. And I want to see how he does."

"If you're still good like you used to be when you was a kid, we're going to see what we can do for you."

I said, "Thank you, baby boy." So me and Jones jumped in the Sanford & Son truck and headed back to the Town Tavern where the rest of the fellas from St. Louis was at. And so I thought it was a good idea to not tell them that Redd was going to give me a shot at the Hacienda because they had treated me so dirty.

And I was the one that got them all out here to Las Vegas and hooked them up with all of the hookups that I remembered from the time I had spent with Sonny to get them auditions. So as we would know it, gratitude got a very short memory. They weren't grateful for nothing that I had done for them. I had cut them records that we brought out here with us. I got us hooked up with different people that I knew before we decided to come out here to Las Vegas. And they didn't even appreciate none of that I had done. And they was so upset that people knew me from the time that I had been out here with Sonny. So I decided to just didn't tell them nothing about where they're going to give me a shot at that Hacienda Hotel.

So that night came. I sneaked off from everybody else and didn't do the show at the Blue Angel. I went down, Jones came and picked me up at the hotel that we were staying and took me to the show. It was so exciting — it was just like you see in the movies. The lights was bright. The girls was fabulous. And the people was looking at me kind of strange because I was dressed real fly. I was dressed in those outfits that Miss Spikes had made me, some special outfits, knowing that I was coming to Las Vegas. (That was my tailor in St. Louis.) And I was looking good. And I had long hair there. And I had finger waves in my hair, and the kick curl in the back.

And we walked into the hotel. People was looking at me because they knew my face, but they weren't sure about who I was, because I had made so much of an impression from when Sonny was alive. And I was walking through the same casino that Sonny and I used to walk through. And a few of those old gangsters recognized me. They spoke to me and hugged me up and stuff. And Jones took me in the back of the showroom where the cast was for the Redd Foxx show.

And the first somebody I think I saw, was Edie Echoes. She sang the Lena Horn type of music. She was a junior graduate. She was very proper and she looked at me as if I had shit on my clothes. You know, like, 'what are you doing back here?' But I didn't pay that no attention because Redd was the boss and Redd had told Jones what to do. And so Jones introduced me to her. She was kind of snotty at that time.

And I met Michael Green. He was the saxophone player in the band with [Calvin] "Eagle Eye" Shields. Eagle Eye Shields was a drummer that used to play with Count Basie, that Redd was as the band leader. And then Jones introduced me to him and told him what Redd had said to put me on. And they looked at Jones like he was crazy, 'just put this kid on?'

And so I saw Prince Spencer. He was one of The Four Stepbrothers. He was the one Stepbrother that was left alive. He was the president of the Redd Foxx Corporation. He was the one that Redd had Told Jones to put me on the stage because Prince ran everything. He is the one that gave me that announcement saying, "Ladies and gentlemen, Redd Foxx is known to put young up-and-coming talent on the stage with him. This is his first opportunity to be on the stage, or any Las Vegas stage. How about a round of applause for Gene Poo Poo Man Anderson..." That was the introduction that Chris gave me after he decided to put me on, after Redd had told him that he'd have to put me on, after he came to the theater.

So everybody was looking at me like, who are you and what you going to do? And I was in the dressing room. I changed and put my uniform that I had in my garment bag and I had put it on. And they was asking me, "Who are you and what's your game? What do you do?"

I said, I'm Gene Anderson, Poo-Poo Man from St. Louis, Missouri. And Redd is going to give me a shot on the show tonight. They looked at me like, 'Redd's going to give you a shot on the show tonight? Who's show? This is our show.' They was awful snotty towards me because they didn't welcome no talent that they didn't know nothing about because this was the big time. But it didn't make no difference to me. I knew that I was qualified to make the audience stand up and applaud for me no matter what time it was, big time or little time. I knew I had it and was 'on time'.

So Jones told Prince, "Redd say put this kid on."

Prince said, "Put him on? I don't know about know nothing about this kid. I wait till Redd get here, pally." That's what Jones called 'em. Prince called everybody pally. "I'll wait till Redd get here, then I'll ask, I'll do what red say do."

Jones said, "Well, I told you he said put him on."

And Prince told him, "I'm not going to put him nowhere until I talk to Redd."

Redd hadn't gotten to the theater yet. So I was standing in the wings watching the show. I saw Edie Echoes, she go out there with her million-dollar gowns on and do the Lena Horn thing. And then I saw The Cherry Blossoms. There was two Oriental girls — they did their little dance routine. And then I saw Eagle Eye Shields in the band. They played their little tune. And then Prince went out there and did his little one-step brother tap dance routine.

And then, next thing I know, Redd went in there and he slapped my hand and they said, "Ladies and gentlemen – two of the funniest words in comedy – how about a round of applause for Redd Foxx?" They put Redd on. And Redd went and did this show. And I stood in the wings and watched Redd do this show. So I figured it was going to bring me on after Redd. I didn't know what was going on.

So Redd did his show and everybody loved it ... and that was it. And I said, damn, I ain't did nothing yet. And Redd came and said, "How did you do, Poo-Poo?"

I said, "They didn't let me get on the stage and do nothing!"

He said, "What?!" He said, "Jones, go and get Prince and tell him I said I want to talk to him."

So Jones went and got Prince and met Prince and said, Prez – he just called Prince Prez – He said, "Prez, didn't I leave a message to let this kid get on?"

Prince said, "Redd, I don't know nothing about this kid. All I know that Jones come talking about putting him on. I don't know what I want to hear from you about that. Don't know nothing about this kid. And this is the big show here. And I want to take a chance on putting on here until I talk to you about it."

So he said, "Well, this is *my* show. And if I said put him on, you put him on." He said, "Matter of fact, I want him to come on tomorrow and put him on before I come on, just before me, 'cause I want him to see his act."

He dais, "Redd, this is the co-star spot — I can't just put him on there, 'cause I don't know nothin' about this kid."

He said, "This is *my* show. If you don't put him on, *everybody* fired." He said, "I want him to do this thing. Cause the kid — I know this kid. I know what he's got."

Prince said, "Well, okay." He say, "Okay, chief."

So he said [to me], "Listen ... those finger waves you got in your hair, here's $100 — I want you to go to them and get them washed out. I want your hair as long as it is; I want it hanging out fucking sling like Cab Calloway." Because I was wearing long white tails back then. And I had a long baton that I used to do my act with. (It's up on YouTube right now, "Redd Foxx and Poo Poo Man, Gene Anderson at the Hacienda Hotel.") That same outfit and that same look and the same show that I had.

So I went home that night and the fellas was upset with me because I didn't make the show that we normally did at the Blue Angel. I still hadn't told them that I had been down there with Redd Foxx. And they was upset with me because they was depending on me 'cause I was young then and I had a lot of energy and I was selling myself so good that everybody wanted to see what I had to offer. I had a fan base that I had developed with those boys from St. Louis from the shows that we had already done. So I wasn't trying to get back with them. I was trying to get over there with Redd.

I had one real friend in the group and that was Lionel Z. Me and him, we the one that got the group together to get them to come to Las Vegas from St. Louis. I told him about the experience over there with Redd Foxx. He said, "Poo Poo, That's a big shot, man. Don't blow it. Go on and do it. Don't worry about us. I'll hold it down on this end."

I said, "Okay Z, I'm going to do it." I couldn't sleep that night. I tumbled and tossed the whole night thinking about my opportunity. It finally came. Sonny tried to get it for me and he died before I could get it. And I tried on my own and couldn't do it. Redd finally came through and he was going to get me a shot on the big stage in Las Vegas with his show.

So that night, I stayed up all night trying to figure out how I was going to approach the show and what kind of act I was going to try to develop for that show. But no rehearsal. I knew that I had a shot and I better do the best I can, to be the best I could ever be. If I was going to ever be good, I was going to have to be that good right there and right then. So I must have prayed all night long. "Lord, please let me be good. Let me have the energy. Let me have all of the skills that I've been taught from all of the people that have gave me some pointers in my life trying to be an entertainer. Let this prove out to be true tomorrow on this show."

The Big Chance

So I finally went to sleep. I must have slept about an hour, I guess. I woke up the first thing in the morning, and I called Jones. Jones came and got me and took me back out to Redd's house. Redd said, "Listen, son, you got a chance to prove yourself on my show. This is a big show. Go out there and do your thing. I know you can do it." Redd was very instrumental in me being motivated because he knew how to motivate me. Because Redd really did love me, and I knew he did.

I remember that Sonny and Redd had a conversation once. We were sitting at the International Hilton Hotel where Redd was performing. And we used to hang out in the International Hotel. Sonny and me used to hang there every day and call that our office. And Redd used to come and sit with us sometime in the lobby. And I remember Sonny and Redd was talking one day in the lobby. Sonny was telling Redd, "If something ever happened to me, I want you to take care of Geney boy." And I happened to walk up and hear him say that.

I said, "What are you talking about if something happened to you?"

He said, "None of your business. And you get on down the road and leave us alone. We know, we grown men talkin'."

I believe Sonny knew that they was trying to get to him and to do something bad to him even back then. And so I remember he told Redd that, and that's what Redd was doing, fulfilling this promise that he had made to Sonny, that he would take care of me. And which he did.

Something did happen to Sonny. I thought about it over and over again that Redd is trying to do something with me. I got to not let him down. I was so excited. Then Jones came and picked me up. We went and had dinner. And we went to the Hacienda again. When I went back,

I had on another one of those fly outfits that Ms. Spikes had made me. And I had my uniform in the garment bag, which, as I said, was white tails and my baton. And everybody was looking at me standing in the wings again. This was the second time I was standing in the wings.

They was laughing at me this time because last time they saw me standing in the wings, I didn't get to do nothing. So this time they was just mocking me because they said, 'this kid here, he's trying to get something going and Redd is just stringing him along'. That's what they was thinking. I knew what they were thinking. I could smell their brains. So I felt that whatever they were thinking, I was going to prove them all wrong because I knew I had what it took. I knew I had stark quality in me, but I just had to get a chance to prove it. And Redd was giving me an opportunity to prove it.

So the show started and Eagle Eye Shields ripped the band off, ba-pabapabapabapabapabopabop! And they did the show as they always did. And then Prince made the announcement. As I said, he said, "Redd Foxx has been known to help up-and-coming young talent on his show. So how about a round of applause for Gene Poo Poo Man Anderson?"

And the band played, dadadada ... and I ran out on the stage and I had already talked to Eagle Eye Shields and told them what I wanted to do. I was going to do *Misty* [Ella Fitzgerald], up tempo, that with the Shuffle. And I was going to do *Let the Good Times Roll*. And I told Eagle Eye, just follow my baton. That's all — just follow my baton. And when I make a break, the band make a break. Eagle Eye and them was such pros.

Eagle Eye, he was on my side, period, because he wanted to see me make it, because he seen it in my heart that I had what it took. Because I think Eagle Eye had seen me at Bob Bayless' joint in Sugar Hill when I was there with Sonny Liston. And so he knew that I had something going for myself as far as being a star.

So he counted it off... "One, two, a one, two, three, four" dotchadot... And I took off running across the stage with that baton in my hand. I had stood in the wings and I prayed — I said, "God, if you're going to ever be good to me, be good to me today." And I ran out there on the stage and I spun around and I started singing, "Look at me, I'm as helpless as a kitten up a tree". And they had never seen nobody do that song up tempo. And I was spinning around and I was real agile.

My ballet dancing as a kid came into handy. And before you know it, the people was grooving with me. They was clapping their hands. And Redd came in. I saw Redd standing in the wings, looking at me, clapping his hands. I knew I had him then. So I went to the next song, *Let the Good Times Roll*. And that's where the baton came in. I was breaking down, "Everybody" Bam! "Let's have some fun!" Bam! "You only live with once, and when you're dead, you're done. Let the good time roll."

And man, that seems to have been my best song because the people got to grooving with it and clapping their hands and they was rolling. I was rolling. I felt good. And the next thing I knew, the women started screaming because I was doing my little gyrations and stuff. And I was getting it on.

So when I finally got off the stage, Redd was standing there and he slapped my hand.

And he ran on the stage, he said, "Ladies and gentlemen, the funniest two words in show business, how about it for Reeeeeeedd Foxx!" And he went out there, dun, dun, dun, dun. He went out there and did his little show. Then when he came back, I had to change clothes and stuff. And I said, "How did you like it, Redd?"

He said, "Man, you still got it, baby boy."

He said, "Matter of fact", he said, "Prince, I told you he had it."

Prince said, "Well, he was a fluke." That's all he said.

"I tell you what, he do the same thing tomorrow. I bet you $50 he do the same thing tomorrow."

And Prince say, "Bet."

So he gave me $100 and said, "Listen, I want you to go — I told you to go and get that hair. I want you to get your hair washed out tomorrow. And so you can sling and take them finger waves out your hair."

And he told Mike, he said, "Mike, I want you to take him to go and get some shoes over to the costume shop because those street shoes that he's wearing is too heavy for him to be dancing like he's dancing. He needs some professional dancing shoes, which is light and they don't weigh nothing. And he can move much better with them."

So that's when me and Mike Green hooked up. We became great friends then because he was a youngster in the band playing saxophone. And he and I was about the same age. So Redd wanted us to kind of like hang out together — because Mike knew the ropes. Because Mike had been on the set a long time with all those old pros. And Mike was teaching me how to do the things that it was necessary to be an old pro in this show business on the strip. So Mike and I became very tight. We used to hang out and do all kinds of things together. We used to knock off girls together and party and carry on and we would smoke that weed and get just funky.

So I went back over to the hotel. I was on top of the world then. To prove myself, to Redd that I still had what it took. And I had been on the stage, the big stage, on the strip. So I said, well, shit, I don't need to go back over there to the Blue Angel with those guys no more. So I stayed over to the hotel by myself. And they asked me where I'd been. I finally broke down and told them what happened. They seemed to be sort of like happy for me, but they was kind of like persnickety about it, because I had to sneak off and did some good for myself. Because they thought that they had me under their fingers. That was a bunch of bull, because I knew that I was going to be on my way now, because I had already proved myself to my old friend Red Foxx.

And the crew knew that they had some brand new life into the show with me. Redd had gave me my big break that I needed, that I was hoping I would get when I left St. Louis. Redd knew he had something special in me because he sent Mike over to the hotel and told Mike to tell me to pack up all my shit and meet him down at the Hacienda in the suite that we used to hang out in. That was our green room more or less, a suite that the hotel had complimented us to stay in and entertain our guests in. So he wanted me to move in there and to get away from those guys because he know those guys didn't mean me no good.

And plus he wanted to groom me himself because he knew that I had something special other than just somebody who could just sing and dance. I had a little charisma that he could use in his show. So I was excited at the fact that Redd had pulled me out of the ghetto and brought me up on the strip where I could really be seen and could do some things where I always wanted to do from the beginning. Even when I was with Sonny, I didn't get that break that Red was able to give me.

So I went back and I did the show that night. I was much better because I was much more relaxed. And I got a standning ovation. Red was so happy. He got the $50 out of Prince. And he said, "Okay, you want to bet again?"

Prince said, "Yeah. He's still a fluke."

He bet Prince again. The next night I did the same thing. And he beat Prince out of $50 again. Then he said, "You want to bet again?"

Prince said, "No, I ain't going to take no chance on letting that son of a bitch break me."

So I start to making a difference in this show.

I finally met her, a lady by the name of Miss Laurie Buckley. She was Lord Buckley's daughter. She was the entertaining editor of the *Vegas Visitor* newspaper. There was a tabloid that reported on all of the acts that was on the strip. And she put me down — she made a flyer that had me down as the co-star of the Redd Foxx Show at the Hacienda.

Boy, that started a riot within our camp because Edie Echoes had been the co-star for years with Redd. And all of a sudden, she had put me down as the co-star. But she didn't know no different because she just saw me come out in that slot a couple times. So when she made the fly up, she just put me in that position where I came in as opening up directly before Redd come on. So that made me the co-star of the show. And that put me in bad with the crew that was in the show. Because here I was, a newcomer on the strip, and nobody never heard of me. And all of a sudden, I'm to co-star the Redd Foxx Show, one of the biggest shows on the strip.

My competition was Ben Vereen. And so everybody, was talking about me. The whole strip was talking about the new guy on the Redd Foxx show, that Poo Poo Man. That word 'Poo Poo Man' — Redd hated it. At that time, he hated that word 'Poo Poo Man'. But Prince had already put it on the introduction tape, so it was out there.

It goes to show you that things happens, and you can't do nothing about it once you got it out there. So Edie Echoes goes to Redd and said, "Redd, I've been with you for too many years, and you're going to let this kid come up there and bump me out of my spot?"

He said, "I'll tell you what I'll do. I'll put you back in your spot, and I'll let him come on just before you do." So he took me out of the cold start spot. I got ready to go before she does, he said, "Go out there and kick that bitch's ass."

And I went out there and I put it down, I put it down, I put it down that night. And when she got through singing, she didn't hardly get any applause at all because I had put it down and I got people screaming and hollering and all for me.

She went back to Redd and said, "Redd, listen, I got things I have to do at night, so you put him back in that spot again because I have to go before it gets too late."

He said, "I told you don't worry about it, didn't I?"

And he put me back in the cold start spot again. So we rode for about a year or so. And then all-of-a-sudden, some people come from Hollywood. Lorimar-Telepicturers came to sign Redd up for a TV series called *Al's Candy Store*. And so they said, "Man, that boy's a phenomenon that you got there. We'd like to have him on our TV show with us."

Redd said, "Yeah, well, you can have him."

And so he came to me and said, "Listen, I got to have a contract on you before I can let you go and get on this TV show with me."

I said, "Yeah, that'd be fine."

So he had – I think the guy name was Philip – he was in the office. He worked in the Redd Foxx office in Hollywood. He drew up a contract and handed it to me. And the contract was so one-sided, it had me giving up all my rights to everything that I was able to do — all my songwriting, all of my book writing, and everything else that I was trying to do at that time would belong to the Redd Foxx Corporation automatically with no negotiation. And I just couldn't sign it.

And Charles Hayes, my friend, I showed it to him. He told me, "Say, listen, sign it, and I'll get you out of it later on."

I said, "I can't do that to Redd. I can't just play him like that."

He said, "Man, sign the contract, Petey." That's what he called me, Petey. He said, "Sign the contract, Petey."

I said, "No, I can't do it, man. I can't sign the contract."

So I didn't sign the contract. So they didn't sign me on as an actor on the TV show. Redd gave me a job, though, on the TV show as camera blocking and his assistant. He never knew. He just thought I just wouldn't sign it. He didn't know nothing about what Phil had put all those different things in the contract that was so derogatory. He never knew that. So he thought I was just being just... smelling myself maybe.

But soon we went to Hollywood. That was my first time being in 20th Century Fox — I think it was 20th Century Fox Studios. I'd never been into a motion picture studio before. And I was so excited. And Redd had me to come out there, and he showed me how to camera-block for him.

He said, "You [about] my complexion and about my height. Say, you'll be a good camera blocker for me."

So he gave me the script, and I did some things in the script. He said, "How would you do this part?" And I tell him how I do that part. And he go out and do it just like I said I would do it. And he said, "You've got to... you're natural, man."

I said, "Damn, I'm a natural." Then for Redd to tell me that, I thought I was on my way. I said, "Man, I've got something going for myself now."

And so Michael Green got jealous. Michael Green went and told Redd, he said, "Redd, Gene Anderson is talking to the producers and directors about different parts of your scenes and stuff." I had spoken to him, but the reason why I spoken to them is because it was some things that they were saying that I knew a little bit better for Redd, than they were saying for Redd. So I just spoke to them and they asked me my opinion. But what nothing wrong with that to be truthful, but that was such a fragile situation, it was best for me not to have had no opinion or had no dialogue with those people at all.

I didn't know that then because I thought me and Redd was cooler than that, but Redd was running scared because it was a new shot since Sanford and Son for him to have a television program. So if I wouldn't have said nothing, I'd have been in good shape because he thought that I might have said something that might have blew his TV shot. But I really didn't mean no harm with my statement because I thought that he had me and Mike there as some of the people that was going to be hanging around in the Al's Candy Store. So we had to have some type of dialogue. I told them we needed some dialogue in the show.

And that would have been good for us to gave us a better shot as being one of the cast members. Instead, he went and hired Sinbad and Vanessa Williams and put them in the show instead of me. So that blew that. So we went on back to the Hacienda and started doing our regular show again.

That's when Frank Sinatra came to see us. We were sitting over there by the Keto machine after the show one night, and a little dude walked over to Redd and he looked awful familiar to me, but I couldn't recognize him. He said to Redd, he said, "Hey, Redd. You got a great show, man." He said, "I love the show. Me and dad came to see your show."

Redd looked at him and said, "I know you kid."

He said, "Yeah, Redd, don't you remember me? I'm the little 'dago' boy that you spanked for stepping on your shoes once."

He said, "Frank Jr."...

"Yeah," he said, "That was Frank Sinatra Jr.. Yeah, me and my sister and my dad and Eddie Pucci, our bodyguard, came down to see your show. We heard you got a Poo Poo Man, and we wanted to know what was a Poo Poo Man."

He said, "The boy's phenomenal." Redd said, "Well, here he is sitting right here." And he introduced me to him. I shook his hand. He said, "Where's Frank [Senior] at?"

He said, "He's over there playing poker." He said [his] dad wanted to meet him too.

And so I said, "Well, I've been a big fan of your dad's all my life."

He said, "Well, he's right over there. Would you like to meet him?"

I said, "Yeah." So he took me over there to meet Frank Sinatra. I shook his hand.

And he said, "Boy, you something special." He said, "Red, he did himself a favor when he got you."

I couldn't believe that was coming from Frank Sinatra's mouth. But that was quite alright with me. So I went back over there to Redd. I was so starstruck by meeting Frank Sinatra. So, he asked me, "Is there any stars you ever met that you really got starstruck by?"

I said, "Yeah."

He said, "Who?"

I said, "Jimmy Reed."

He said, "Jimmy, who?"

I said, "Jimmy Reed, the blues singer."

He bust out laughing. I must he thought I was going to say somebody like Sammy Davis, Jr., but Sammy was my idol though.

But it was Jimmy Reed. Jimmy Reed was so impressive to me because he talked just like he sang. And I was so influenced by Jimmy Reed as a youngster coming up. My mother then bought so many of his records and stuff that I always wanted to meet him. And then when I did get to meet Jimmy Reed, I was so impressed with that he was so authentic. It was hard to believe that someone could be that themselves. That was Jimmy Reed.

So time went on. Years passed by. We did our show. The *Al's Candy Store* came out. It lasted a little while — it didn't last long. Then we was hanging around and all of a sudden a guy came up to me, a little guy came up to me and said, "Hey, I'd like to meet Mr. Redd Foxx. Eddie Murphy sent me over here to meet him." I can't think of his name right now. He was Eddie Murphy's right-hand man. And he said he wanted to talk to Redd about doing a show, doing a movie called *Harlem Nights*.

I said, "Redd needs to talk to those youngsters." Red didn't even want to talk to him. I said, "Let me talk to Redd about it." So I went and talked to Redd about it. I said, "Redd, Eddie Murphy sent this youngster over here to talk to you about doing a movie called *Harlem Nights*." I said, "Redd, you ought to do this movie because those youngsters got something going on. Eddie Murphy and them, they doing some big things."

He said, "I don't want to fool with those guys."

I said, "Redd, please, listen to him."

He said, "Well, you tell him I said send Eddie over here to talk to me."

So I told the dude that. He went on back, and he went and got Eddie. And Eddie came and talked to Redd about doing *Harlem Nights*. And Redd decided to do it since Richard Pryor was in it. Richard Pryor used to stay in Redd's trailer in the back of Redd's nightclub. So Redd was kind of partial to Richard Pryor. So he took the script and he decided to do the movie *Harlem Nights*.

Red's House Parties

Every so often, Redd would have an idea of pulling everybody together and have a house party over to his home. Something was so unique about Red's House Party was that Redd had a one-way mirror in his bedroom that led out to the living room. You could see out into the living room, but you couldn't see into the bedroom. Redd had all kinds of little funny gadgets in his house that he would be able to spy on people and see what they were doing in his house. They wouldn't have the slightest idea that he was aware of what was going on.

He would love to cook. For two or three days, he would cook food for his guests and line up all kinds of activities. When it was time for the party, he would be the only person that didn't show up for the party.

He would invite some of his friends, like Eagle Eye Shields, the drummer [in] his show. He would invite Prince Spencer, who was one of the four stepbrothers who was the president of our organization, the Redd Foxx Corporation. He would invite Cha Cha Hogan, who was a member of the Ink Spots singing group. Those were his personal people. And he would invite a lot of young ladies that were dancers at the Hacienda, as well as stars like Esther (Lawanda Page).

He would invite Lyn Roman. She was a big-time singer back in those days. She had a lot of sisters, and Redd used to love them. So he would have me come over and help him cook for the guests that were going to be at the party.

He would hire a DJ to play the music so people could party and dance-off. He would always ask me, "Who was having the most fun out there?" Talking about the people that was in the backyard by the swimming pool, and the people that was in the living room. He wanted to know who was having a good time. He would hit me on my page and have me come back there and talk about it to him, and tell him who was having the most fun. He was strange with that. He wanted everybody to have a good time, and didn't want to be there at his own party.

That used to freak me out, because I said, "Red, all you got to do is just walk out the bedroom and go into the party."

He said, "No, I just want everybody to have a good time. It ain't about me, it's about y'all."

He was very thoughtful about who was enjoying themselves and who wasn't. Redd was more than a congenial type of person. He would do that and spend hundreds of dollars, sometimes a grand, to make his parties successful — and would never walk out of the bedroom. I couldn't understand that.

But sooner or later, he would always emerge out of the bedroom at the end of the party when just about a few people was left. And they would be so glad to see him. And he would get on my ass. It seemed like he just waited for the time to get on my ass about my act in front of all those people. And he said, "Poo Poo, you ain't strutting right."

I said, "What you mean, I ain't strutting right?"

A strut is the dance that you walk with your hand in the air, and you wave them up and down, and step it high. Like a drum major. You know the guy that leads the band in a parade? That's strutting.

So he said, "Prez, you show Poo Poo how to strut." So Prince starts strutting around the swimming pool.

And now, everybody's eyes was on me. They said, "You get out there and you do it now." So I started trying to copy what Prince was doing. And I started strutting.

And Redd said, "No, that ain't right."

I was doing the same thing Prince was doing, but I musta didn't have the swagger. Because Redd would get on my ass like a duck on a junebug. He said, "No, that ain't right. You ain't strutting with the authority of the strut. And that's very important to you and your show. Because you've got something that a lot of youngsters will never have."

That's when I found out that he really was paying attention to me and developing me to be a major star in his show.

So he told Eagle Eye, he said, "Listen, when you go, you take him home with you. And I want you to make him strut all the way in everything y'all do. You go to the store or you go up and down the hallways. I want him strutting in the house all the way. Don't let him walk. Just make him strut. Because he's got to perfect that strut. Because that's what working his act so good. And you know I want to see him make it to the top."

So Eagle Eye, after the party was over, made me go to his house and stay with him one day in order for me to perfect that strut. He made me strut up and down the streets. He made me strut in the house. He made me strut everywhere I went. I had to strut. I wasn't walking — I was just strutting. And I finally got it down pat. He said, "Now you got it."

So the next day, we went back to the grind of the show. And when my part came out, I did the strut. Everybody was watching me to see was I going to strut in the right way. And so I smoothly stepped high like a majorette. And I started to strut. And man, everybody was watching me. I could feel their eyes on me to see was I doing it right.

And Red, after I did my act and came off the stage, Redd grabbed me and hugged me and said, "You got it, boy. Listen. Listen to 'em applaud. Listen to 'em." Because they was waiting on me to do the strut.

I didn't know that. All the audience seemed like they had been at the party and seen them teach me how to strut. Because when I started strutting across the stage, everybody just, the audience just exploded with applause and laughter. That's when I knew I found a brand new arsenal to project my show. That strut was a powerful tool that I didn't know the importance of it back when I first started doing it. But after the experience with Eagle Eye, I was able to be able to do that strut with ease.

Another thing I remember that Redd brought to me concerning my act, he said, "Listen, you ain't got your act together."

I said, "What you mean?" I said, "The people is going crazy. They screaming and carrying on and wanting more."

He said, "That ain't it. You don't have your act together."

I said, "What you mean, Redd?" once again.

He said, "I want you to have your eyes in the same spot every night. I want you to have your foot in the same spot every night. I want you to have your hands in the same spot every night. That's when you got to act."

Then I understood what he was meaning when he said that. To tell the truth, I got so much out of Redd that he wanted me to know he was just, he must have felt that something was going on in his life that he wanted me to be a part of it, and some big things should have happened for me.

So we went back to Hollywood. And I was commissioned to make an album out of some old scraps that he had, a box of them. He said, "Poo Poo, I want you to put me an album together that don't have no cursing in it."

I said, "Redd, that's almost impossible to do."

He said, "Yeah, well, you go through all these tapes and you edit out me an album."

So I started going through all the tapes and I found some spots where he was just commenting and making gestures, and that was funny enough because Redd was funny no matter how you put it. So I put the album together and let him hear it. He just died laughing.

He said, "Boy, you know how to do that thing, don't you?" (Talking about editing.)

I said, "Yeah, Redd, I did this all my life."

He said, "I'll tell you what, I want you to cut a record for me — a record called *Exactly Like You*."

And I cut that record for him and he loved it. And he said, "Man, you a diamond in the rough. You everything I've been needing." That's when he made me the vice president of his record company, Ready Freddie Records. He got me some cards made and everything. I was passing them out. The Redd Foxx company, Ready Freddie Records, was getting the name out all over Hollywood. I was passing them out like confetti.

Speaking of the cards, one day I was cutting across a lot trying to get home to my apartment and I passed through an In-N-Out Burger, and I walked through a section where they would order their food in the car. And there in an old Plymouth was Bob Hope and his wife. I couldn't believe it. So I knocked on the window and he rolled the window down. He said, "What can I do for you, son?"

I said, "You Bob Hope, ain't you?"

He said, "Yeah."

I said, "I'm a big fan of yours... I work for Redd Foxx." And I gave him one of those Ready Freddie cards, and he grabbed it and he laughed his ass off.

He said, "Redd finally found somebody that can do something with that old raggedy ass record company, ain't he?"

I said, "Yeah, I just cut him a record called *Exactly Like You*."

And he bust out laughing, and he said, "What is Redd up to now?"

I said, "He's fixing to do a movie. Eddie Murphy and them sent some people over there for him to do a movie called *Harlem Nights*, but Redd don't want to talk to 'em. I'm going to have to get on his ass and make him talk to these guys because Eddie Murphy and them don't be jiving. They got some big-time things going on and Redd need to get with them youngsters and do some fresh stuff."

He said, "You're right about that. You tell Redd to call me", and he gave me a number. He said, "Tell Redd to call me."

And I said, "I'm glad to do that."

So we chit-chatted about little things here and there. I asked him about Bing Crosby and he said Bing Crosby was his greatest friend throughout his whole lifetime in the show business. I said, "I used to try to sing like Bing Crosby when I was a kid." He bust out laughing.

So I got a relationship with Bob Hope from that day on. We used to talk occasionally. I used to call that number he gave me. Bob Hope was a very unique person as well as Redd. All them old guys had a uniqueness about them, an aura that was unexplainable. They had something that was so special and Bob Hope was no different. He had something special, too.

So somehow we was at the show and Eddie Murphy sent one of his henchmen to the show to see if he could get Redd to sign a contract to do *Harlem Nights*. And Redd wouldn't sign it. Redd wouldn't even talk to the youngster. Redd said, "You send Eddie Murphy and tell him to come talk to me himself about that movie if he wants me to do it." So the guy must have went back to Eddie and told him that.

One day we looked up at the Hacienda behind the stage. That was Eddie Murphy. He went to the dressing room and him and Redd, they laughed and they talked. And he introduced me to Eddie. And Eddie turned out to be real cool. He wasn't stuck up like I thought he would have been. He was a big star as far as I was concerned. But to Red, he was just another youngster just doing something. And so they finally came to an agreement that Redd would do the movie.

I was so happy. Knowing that Richard Pryor was in the movie and a bunch of other big-name stars was in the movie, it was going to be a great movie. And I was going to get a chance to go back to Hollywood with Redd and to see how the thing was done.

Man, I was so excited for him. But about that time, the IRS was all over him. They was trying to take the building. They then took the mansion in Chadsworth, California. And they was trying to get his house, the one in Las Vegas. They was trying to just take everything from Red. And it was heartbreaking to see him suffer like that. The man had worked his whole life to get a few things that he deserved in being a star. And the IRS was just going to just take it from him — just gangster this stuff. And it was frustrating him so bad. He was consistently stressed out about the IRS. He bought a brand new car.

He bought a Zimmerman. I think it was a Zimmerman. And it used to talk. It used to say, "You're too close to me. You're standing too close to me." And that's what the car was speaking. And I loved the car.

And he said, "They're going to come and take this car too, it looks like."

I said, "Well, Red, all you got to do is just drive the car across the stage and say you need it as a prop, and they can't take the car."

He didn't pay me no attention because he thought I was just a youngster, didn't know nothing about nothing except dancing and singing. But if he would have listened to me, he would have still had all that stuff because I was going to make a school out of the building for up-and-coming young talent on the different floors where you had the studio... You had the motion picture editing studio and all of that. They used to do that. And they used to do screening of new movies in this theater that he had on the second floor. I had the first floor as my studio for recording and to do my little thing, when I used to stay in there when I went to Hollywood with Redd.

As time went on, it was time to shoot the movie, *Harlem Nights*. I used to go to the studio of the Paramount Motion Pictures to see them shoot some scenes. Eddie Murphy and I used to chitchat occasionally. But the person I used to talk to was a guy by the name of Danny Aiello, a major actor that was in *Harlem Nights*. He played the police that was a nemesis of Eddie Murphy.

I used to talk to Richard Pryor sometimes. And he was from Peoria, Illinois, which was down the street from my hometown, St. Louis, Missouri. And we used to kick it and laugh. Richard Pryor was a great person. He was sort of like a little sick during that time. I don't know what was wrong with him, but he was a little sick. And off camera, he would start shaking, like nerves. But on camera, he would be composed. I don't know how he was able to do it, but Richard Pryor was a strong man to have been able to survive what I thought I saw him going through at that time.

I looked at the set. Eddie was directing, and he was acting at the same time. He is so brilliant. I couldn't believe that he was just that smart. But he know he had to have it about making motion pictures, though. And they were sharp every day.

I used to talk to Della Reese. She liked me. She thought I was a decent young man. And she used to tell Redd, "You do something with this kid, because he's got some talent. And he's somebody."

And Redd used to laugh and say, "Oh, that's Poo Poo. That's my baby boy. I'll take care of him. Don't worry about it."

So eventually, the movie came out. It was a big success. I went to see it at Grandma's Chinese Theater in Hollywood. Redd was on top of the world. Everything was going great for him.

All of a sudden, Eddie Murphy came up with an idea from the scenes that Redd and Della Reese had, the magic that was in the movie. So he put them together and came up with a series called The Royal Family. It was a TV series. And we used to go to the set that was shooting over, I think it was still over Paramount. I used to go over there every day trying to learn something, trying to meet some people. I walked into an office where Henry Winkler, 'The Fonz', had an office. And I tried to talk to him about trying to get into the movies. I was trying to talk to anybody, because I was trying to get a shot in the movies.

| 168 | - RED'S HOUSE PARTIES

Alone in Hollywood

So one day, as time had rolled around, I had gotten in trouble in Hollywood, because I wasn't doing no singing, no nothing at that time, just trying to hang around Redd at the motion picture lot. And I had gotten into a situation where I was on probation, and I had missed my parole officer appointment. So they had a warrant out for my arrest, and I didn't even know it. So I was going across the street, and I jaywalked, and the police stopped me and asked my identification. And I showed it to him, and he checked it and found out that I was wanted for a parole violation.

So they locked me up. And in going to jail, I had a chance to make one phone call. So I called over Paramount and asked to speak to Redd. And I think it was Danny Aiello that picked up the phone and was talking to me and said, "Well, Redd is dying in the middle of the floor."

I said, "What you mean Redd's dying in the middle of the floor?"

"He had a heart attack, and the paramedics are with him right now."

I almost had a heart attack myself by hearing that about Red. I knew how he was. And the IRS had been on him and stressed him out. He couldn't take stress bad. He used to break out in hives when he'd get stressed out like that.

So I was trying to get out, and I had to go to court a couple days later about my parole violation. And I was trying to get out in order to see about Redd, and there was no kind of way that I could manage to make it out of jail. I went to court, and the judge asked me how did I plead. I pleaded no contest, hoping that I could get it right out and make it to the funeral.

But they instead, they kept me for another two weeks, and I missed the funeral. And Redd's people never did forgive me for missing the funeral, because they figured if anybody should have showed up, it should have been me. But I couldn't do nothing about it, because I was in jail.

So everybody told me about the funeral. After I got out of jail, I was so sad. That was my last hope, because Sonny had died on me, Redd had died on me, and I was all alone in Hollywood. And I flew around there some kind of way and got into the streets, and I started doing all kind of crazy shit that I should have never dreamed about that I would be doing at this time in my life. I was a star, and I flew around there, was in the streets gangbanging, selling dope, doing all kind of crazy shit. And it just seemed like there was no end to it. It was horrible doing those things. I was pimping and everything else I could do to stay alive, sleeping outside sometimes.

I used to hang out with a guy by the name of Ed Townsend. He wrote that song, *Let's Get It On*, for Marvin Gaye. And Big Ralph was my homeboy. And they used to take care of me at the hotel in Hollywood where the stars used to hang out. I was hanging out with James Caan, the movie star. New gossip, another movie star. I was hanging out with nothing but the stars, but I was still doing the wrong thing. I wasn't concentrating on my singing. I wasn't concentrating on my stage action. All I was concerned with was trying to stay high and trying to forget about Sunny being dead and Redd being dead, and I was all alone in Hollywood. I was trying to do all kind of things that was derogatory towards my being a star that I had once been.

All I was thinking about was just survival. I started hanging out with Rick James and hanging out with Charlie Wilson. Before you know it, I was locked up in jail again. They sent me to CRC [California Rehabilitation Center]. I was there with Rick James and Ike Turner and a lot of other stars that had fell by the wayside just like I had. All I knew was that I had to redeem myself some kind of way.

My mother died while I was in the penitentiary. My great-aunt Bessie died while I was in the penitentiary. All these people that died while I was in jail and I was disgraced by letting my career fall apart after all the work that Redd and Sunny had put into me, because I had a dope habit that was from here to Moscow.

I couldn't shake it and I knew I said "Jesus!" I fell on my knees and I said, "Jesus, you can help me. You can take this dope habit from me and get me back started. Nobody can do it but you, Lord."

Somehow I messed up and they put me in the hole and I started thinking. I was thinking about my mom had died and it was hurting me so bad that she had died when I was in the penitentiary. I knew that the only way that I was going to get back was to forget about the dope, forget about the street life, forget about the pimping, forget about anything that had nothing to do with entertaining and I could be able to redeem myself. So I prayed and I prayed hard for God to forgive me for all of the injustice that I had done to my life, and he had gave me so much talent.

And so I said, "Jesus, you can do it. You know you can do it."

That meant that the only thing that I had to do was just to try to get me some records. So I called Willie Mitchell when I got out. I told him what kind of experiences I had been going through and he was an old friend of mine. He said, "You come down here in Memphis, Tennessee, and I'll cut you some more records and get you back started."

So I caught a plane and I went down to Memphis, Tennessee, and I cut a record called *Could I, Would I, Should I*. It became a pretty decent hit record, and it was one of the greatest records I had ever written. And so I sing this song right now, "Could I, Would I, Should I..." And it does me good — it reflects on my entire life, and all the things that I had done wrong, and some of the things that I had done right.

So I finally came back to Las Vegas.

I went to see Red's grave.

I went to see Sonny Liston's grave.

Epilogue

And that was the story. Sonny was buried right down the street from Redd's house. I rode down to the cemetery where Sonny was buried, I looked for Sonny everywhere I couldn't find him. I went and asked the caretaker two or three times, "Where's Sonny Liston buried?"

They say, "He's buried right ova' there. Right behind you."

And I still didn't see him, I started to cryin'. I said, "Damn, I say, man, Sonny... I can't find you, man, I want to see you so bad."

I got ready to leave and I stumbled backwards, over a headstone that said

Charles 'Sonny Boy' Liston
1932-1970
"A Man"

That was Sonny's grave. I was still cryin' and I said, "Sonny, you would even trick me, even in your death. Even at yo grave sight, you dirty bastard, you." And I bust out laughin' and went on home. And that was the story of Sonny and me.

- Gene Anderson, aka 'Poo Poo Man' of the George Clinton Parliament Funkadelic / P-Funk Allstars.

ALSO BY GENE ANDERSON

Available at TheGeneAndersonStory.Com